ANGEL TIMELINES

CATHERINE LANIGAN

Cat Nolan Publishing

512 Andrew Avenue #211

La Porte, IN. 46350

Cataloging-in-Publication Data for this title is available through the Library of Congress.

ISBN: 979-8-218-97333-9 (print)

Printed and bound in the United States by Amazon Kindle, Inc.

To contact the author of this book: www.catherinelanigan.com

@cathlanigan on Twitter and Facebook.

Dedication

This book is dedicated to my beloved mother, Dorothy Lanigan, who died on June 12, 2011; to my sweet sister, Nancy Jean Lanigan Porter, who died on May 7, 2009 and to my beloved father, Frank J. Lanigan, who died on Valentine's Day, 1992.

Thank you for being my angels standing by me.

Angel Timelines

INTRODUCTION

*I*n the matrix of divine consciousness, there is no time. Time exists on earth. This book is a collection of timeless stories of angelic intercession in human lives. Some stories go back fifty years or more. Some are recent angel sightings during the Covid-19 pandemic and now post-pandemic.

Though the world appears bleak according to mainstream media news outlets, or propaganda venues, the truth is that the Beings of Light, Celestial Angels, and Divine Messengers have never been this active in human life. Even at that two-thousand year ago point in history's convergence of Hellenistic beliefs, Jewish Mysticism and an array of religions, that gave way to the spiritual need to thrust back the evil forces that threatened to drown mankind once and for all; at the very time of the Christ-consciousness making its appearance at Bethlehem, and who brought the good news of a merciful, all-powerful God which created a world of perfect forms—Human Forms; Divine intervention (for the Western world) was contained in the Middle East—Jerusalem and later Greece.

Today, Celestial Beings of Light, Alpha Angels, Warrior Angels and the highest frequency inter-dimensional Spiritual Beings, whose intentions are guided by God/One Source/ The Creator solely to aid humanity in its ascent to higher consciousness/Christ consciousness and to a world of peace, harmony, love, mutual respect, and kindness; these angels abound in fantastical numbers. The stories here will attest to that fact.

Stop and think about it.

What a world we would have if we were all simply kind to each other! Not just occasionally but daily. Even hourly.

From our origins, we have been programmed to believe we are separate from Source, our Creator. We in the western world have been told we were born with sin. In the east, Hindus and Buddhists believe that their karma and this world is one of suffering and pain. We have all been operating under the illusion and delusions that we are separate from Source. Few, except the very enlightened and knowledgeable, understand that humanity exists in a high state of consciousness. We have not just a soul but a Divine Spark of God within us.

Everything that we want to know about us, our origins, who we are and the power we wield is within us. What has happened over these millennium is that we have forgotten how to access our inner being.

Our destiny is to find our way back to Source—to create the Kingdom of Heaven on Earth and that time is now. This timeline in which we find ourselves, as harrowing as the fake media and government dictators would have us believe, is a miracle point in human history. We can master this matrix and create that kingdom of peace and harmony.

We have been taught to believe that we are separate races based on religions, nationalities, and skin tint. But that is not the truth.

We are ALL the HUMAN Race.

Just as Angels are the Angelic race.

Just as Beings from other planets are Pleiadians, Arcturians, and so on; and though each of those races are not human, we all share the same galaxy and Universe. We are not separate from them any more than we are separate from God or the Angels.

We humans access our God Spark each time we experience the majesty, depth, and breadth of our caring and ability to love. Humans are lovers. We love plants, animals, the earth, sky, and sea. We have compassion for the less fortunate and even for our enemies.

We are the only ones who are going to save ourselves from the evil that THINKS it is going to win the war over our souls. But Evil is wrong.

We have guidance from Angels and Source/God.

We have only to LISTEN. Unfortunately, few of us are doing that. We pretend or convince ourselves that our intuition is imagination. We disregard divine interventions as coincidences. We ignore the goosebumps on our skin when we hear the truth. We tell ourselves that the symbolisms in our dreams are just a cartoon; much like a make-believe Disney princess. We explain away our dreams as not real. For fear of not being "normal" or not "fitting-in" to our social groups, we ignore scientific and spiritual research, revelations and discoveries that explain the matrix we live in and how this 3D reality is not all there is to life.

There are innumerable timelines we could explore but that would take volumes. The basic three are:

Truth time (the true reality of all life) is the frequency (963 Htz) in which The Source/God exists. (Also referred to as heaven).

Earth time is the 3rd dimension matrix or illusion. This earth---this illusion, this matrix can be escaped.

Reality is the life that exists on timelines and dimensions outside the box of earth time and space.

We are being given the chance to open our eyes. To finally wake up, and pay attention to our personal angels and guides who visit us nightly, daily, in the car; through familiar and haunting songs on the radio that resonate to a person dead or alive that we know. These divine beings are pushing us more than ever because the timeline we have created here on earth is ending.

A new time is dawning. Quantum Physics has proven that behind the matrix that holds all creation together is Divine Consciousness. With our hearts we can see this is true. Not with the mind, controlled by past and present un-truths.

The truth---the timeline of the end of the sufferings, war, want, and ignorance is unfolding faster than many humans can absorb. It is Divinely presented to you as a Gift straight from Our Creator. Angels. Ascended Masters. Jesus. Mother

Mary. Archangel Michael. Moses. Figures from the Bhagavad Gita and the Kabbalah. They are all the same Divine Spirit coming to bring you happiness and joy.

Still cannot see it? That is what this book is for. Here you will see the ways in which angels come through the dimensions to enlighten us. You will learn how to pay attention to signs that the divine is close to you. You will learn how to travel through the timelines, unimpeded using meditation.

This book is not a scientific documentary, though I have consulted science through my own research and I urge you to do the same. At this time in our history, we are seeing science, religion, psychology, and metaphysics blending to bring clarity and understanding to who we are.

The answers to all we need to know are inside us. Our soul/brain/cell memory is a storehouse of all knowledge. This is a large part of our God Spark. When we realize that we are co-creators with Source, we understand we create the world we want to live in. Our thoughts are powerful. If you think the world is a place of war, hatred, and violence, you will create that for yourself. If you think in terms of lack; that is what you will receive.

These stories here, come to you from my interaction with ordinary people like you, coming forward and sharing their experience. I have great gratitude to you all; both for sharing and for being courageous enough to read.

One

YOU DON'T BELIEVE IN ANGELS, DO YOU?

Author Note: This story here is presented because the frequency and astrological placements of 2008 are similar, if not spot on, to the frequencies of 2024.

I was in New York City in September of 2008 when Lehman Brothers filed for bankruptcy and the stock market crashed. I was staying at a bed and breakfast in Connecticut only a commuter train ride away from the city. Within forty-eight hours of the announcement from Lehman Brothers, the newscasts predicted nothing but economic gloom. Within that same time frame, the townspeople of Old Greenwich were already talking about the loss of property values, the slowdown in the tourist trade and the lack of retail sales that would annihilate and destroy their lives as they had known it. As I look back, I am not surprised at their reactions. For years too many Americans had watched perfectly acceptable older homes that most of us grew up in, bulldozed to rubble and huge, poorly designed, and most often rather ugly, monstrosities of brick, stucco and wood take their places. Where once there was charm in the beach towns and villages along Long Island Sound, now were "Mac Mansions" owned by Wall Street traders and brokers, CEOs of companies that had swindled their investors and supporters.

We all knew the "bubble" ride of insane housing prices and both personal and government spending could not last.

It did not.

With the collapse of overblown institutions came the revelations of the names of the swindlers and the crooks who escaped the debacle with their corporate multi-million dollar "golden parachutes."

Little did we know then how truly deep the wound the debacle and scandal of Freddie Mac and Freddie Mae would slice into the lives of the American people.

In that week I went to meetings in Manhattan and the "talk" everywhere was about the coming recession. The word "Depression" was spoken much too often in the delicatessens in the Bronx and along the sidewalks in Times Square. I could literally feel the fear slipping in and out of conversations and I saw it in the eyes of a bookseller in Old Greenwich.

Ironically, I was in Manhattan pitching my next collection of true angel stories to publishers. In one meeting an editor said to me, "You don't actually think people believe in angels, do you?"

Another editor said, "Angel books do not sell. I am not interested."

To put it mildly, I was stunned. I was coming close to wanting to stand next to the bronze statue of George M.

Cohan in Times Square and give extemporaneous lectures about angels and their existence among us.

I had just walked out of another publishers' offices in lower Manhattan when my cell phone rang. It was my agent.

"Where are you?"

"In New York."

"Run, do not walk to the nearest kiosk or newsstand, and get a copy of *USA Today*. On the front page is a huge story about angels! It gives the statistics about the number of Americans who believe in God and angels."

"Today? Of all days, while I am pitching this book?"

"The country is going down the tubes by the second. The market is still plummeting. We heard on the news some stock trader jumped off the Empire State Building. Did you hear that?"

"No. But it would not surprise me. People here are scared. If ever there was a time that people needed true stories about real angels, this is it. I am truly blessed," I smiled to myself, saying a quick "thank you" to my angels.

I hung up and rushed to a nearby newsstand. I picked up the *USA Today* and sure enough, on the lower half of the front page was a huge story about Americans' belief in God and angels.

Some of the most interesting statistics were:

96% of people believe in God (microcase Study 2002)

79% of Americans believe in miracles

93% of households have a Bible

72% of Americans believe in Heaven

82% of Americans are conscious of the presence of God

95% of Americans have experienced God's presence or a spiritual force that felt very close to them.

There were a lot more statistics in the Gallup Poll, but the bottom line was that 6 in 10 Americans believe that religion is very important in our lives. That same number of Americans believe that religion and our spiritual life can solve the problems of today.

As I remember that sunny, golden September afternoon in New York, as I looked down at that newspaper headline, I can feel the awe that flooded me at the time. What were the chances that I would be in New York to experience one of the most shocking, frightening times of the new century? Had it been Black Friday in 1929, historically, this day ran an exact parallel. Fortunes had been lost. Corporations toppled. Soon, companies would be closing. People would lose their homes. The numbers of homeless would increase and stretch already tight budgets at Family Shelters to the breaking point.

The stories of our parents' and grandparents' trials and struggles to endure the Great Depression are the underpinnings of our sub-conscious. Films, photographs, and television shows remind us in harrowing clarity the plight of the Plains farmers, the desperate out-of-work dock workers and manufacturing laborers who worked for ten cents an hour. All of us can lay claim to a Pulitzer Prize winning story of courage and soul-testing times that our ancestors endured during the 1930's.

Nothing brings a human being closer to God than to be on his knees. Once we are knocked down, we all seem to find the time to pray. On our knees we plead for God's help. On our knees we ask for forgiveness.

On our knees we find our spiritual self.

What is there about human beings that we seem to take all the credit for the good things that happen in our lives, yet we blame God and the divine for the bad times?

If you ask me, it is conceit. Maybe it is jealousy. Are we so jealous of God and all that he/she/they can do, that we cannot stand it that they get all the credit? We try to take some of God's credit away and say, "I built my corporation with my own bare hands. It is my name on the tallest building in the world. I have a Mansion in Connecticut. I did it all by myself."

I do not think it works that way.

Neither do the hundreds upon hundreds of people writing to me and sending me their real experiences. We believe there is something else going on. And apparently, according to the Gallop Poll, most Americans believe that God is the force behind all our progress, and the fact that we have been a nation at (relative) peace since World War II.

When I began to write my very first angel book, I believed my mission would begin and end with that book. I was wrong. For those of you who do not know my personal story, I will tell it to you briefly, because it is important for you all to understand why I do this.

My father, Frank Lanigan, was an attorney; graduated at the top of his class from Notre Dame Law School. He was Phi Beta Kappa. He had a photographic memory. I worked in his law offices for five years while in high school and college and I can attest to the man's ability to remember something he read in a law journal thirty years prior. He could quote the law verbatim and tell me on which page in the journal I would find the law and in which paragraph on the page. My father was the most intelligent man I had ever met.

My father had a heart attack at the Grand Canyon back in the late 1980's. He was dead for twenty-two minutes. When he came back from death, my sister, Nancy, (who was also a witness to this event) and I flew to Flagstaff to the ICU to see him. He said to me, "Cath, I have to tell you what they told me on The Other Side."

He proceeded to tell me that a "Being of Light" told him that my mission on earth was to chronicle stories of people who had met with or had seen an angel. I was not to judge, criticize, categorize, or try to interpret anything. Just write those stories down.

There is a great deal more to the story, which I have related in my other books, but you get the idea.

At the time I could not help thinking, "Where in the world am I going to find enough kooks like me who think they have seen an angel?" Besides, most people do not want other people to know that they have seen Jesus or an angel for a great many reasons. Once you get a reaction like, "What makes you so special that you have seen an angel and I haven't," it pretty much makes you shut down.

In addition, my own experiences, while exceptional to me, would only fill a very small journal. Not a whole book.

My surprise came only a few days later when I went to the Grand Canyon with my sister, Nancy, and had my first experience with "slipping in time." That is what I called the event, though perhaps, "crossing into another dimension" or "falling into the past," might be more accurate. While looking at the layers of rock and shale in the canyon walls, I suddenly witnessed the air and sunlight altering right before my eyes. The air seemed denser and the slant of the light, more golden as if the light were being sifted through dry dust particles. My clothes had altered to a long white linen skirt and white shirt with long sleeves. On my head was a straw hat with long black, grosgrain ribbons. On my feet were high topped boots that pinched my toes. I heard a horse whinnying behind me where before there had been not even a road, just a walkway. I heard the crunching sound that wooden wagon wheels make on gravel.

"Cath, are you alright?" Nancy asked me.

I heard trepidation in her voice. I did not turn my eyes away from the canyon wall far in the distance. "Sort of. Why?"

Nancy's hand reached out for me. I had my hand on the stone waist-high wall that was in front of me. Suddenly, Nancy's hand was covered in a white lace, finger-less glove. It was if her hand slipped through the dimensions to where I was. She clutched at my hand. Hard.

"Cath, we should go in and get something to eat."

"Why? I'm not hungry."

"You look pale. We are getting something to eat."

Then it was over. It was only about forty-five seconds. It could not have been a whole minute, but it was real. Unnervingly real.

Time switched back to the present.

Nancy nearly dragged me toward the lodge. We were seated immediately near an impossibly huge glass wall that looked out over the Grand Canyon. The lodge had been built in 1903, which was precisely the year I thought I had "slipped back" to.

Nancy was trembling as she looked at me. Then I realized she was checking me out like I was some kind of specimen.

"You won't believe what happened to me," I said.

"Yes, I will."

I shook my head. "Not this one. It is wild. And if you did believe me, it is just because you are my sister and you love me."

"I'll believe it."

I explained to Nancy what happened, including the part where her hand had slipped through the dimensions.

She took a sip of her tea and nodded. "It's the truth."

I was surprised that she was taking me at my word so completely. Frankly, I was in disbelief myself. "I still find it hard to believe."

Her eyes were unwavering as she said, "Cath, you did not just look pale. You were transparent."

I almost thought I did not hear her correctly. "Transparent?"

"Uh, huh. I could see right through you. I reached for you because I knew you were going away and I did not want to lose you."

I was in shock at what she was saying because it all rang true, and by this time we were both shaking and crying.

To this day, I still do not know exactly what happened. I figure that sometime on my travels with book tours and with meeting so many interesting people, I will come across a quantum physics professor who might have a scientific answer.

I have a romantic answer that has to do with love and souls and one that I have come to believe, but that explanation would be wrapped around my grief over Nancy's death years ago.

My mind, heart and gut tell me that in that moment at the Grand Canyon, I was moving through a "veil." It probably was not The Veil, but a portal, an energy grid, perhaps the next dimension. The fact was, I went somewhere out of this time, but in the same space. I was transparent. Where did my body go? What was Nancy seeing? She was my witness.

It was Nancy who reached out to me and kept me on the earth or in this dimension. Here it is, decades later and she is dead and in heaven or the next dimension and I am on earth. She loved me enough to risk her own being at the time. I cannot believe for an instant that Nancy knew any more than I did what was happening. But her love for me caused her to risk her own life in the unknown to save me. Wherever I was, that is where she wanted to be. She did not take the time to think it through. She did not use logic or reason. She acted on the knowledge of her heart. She used love as her guide.

This story about Nancy and me at the Grand Canyon is important for you to know, because in this book you are going to read several stories about Nancy's apparitions and communications to me and others after her death on May 7, 2009.

During one of Nancy's hospitalizations when she was battling cancer, she was demanding several "death bed promises" from me. Finally, I said, "Okay. Fine. But you must promise me that you will communicate with me from The Other Side. You must talk to me."

Nancy clamped her mouth shut and would not answer.

I did not know if it was because she did not believe she was going to heaven, or if she was just so "done" with life on earth she did not want anything more to do with any of us.

I demanded, "You were the one who kept me on earth to be with you when I could have left. Promise me."

I could not imagine one minute of my life without Nancy in it and I knew that if she promised, she would keep her promise. She always did.

"I promise. I will," she said looking away from me.

"Don't you be crossing your fingers to nix this," I joked.

She laughed and said, "It's a promise."

As you read the stories about Nancy in this book, you will see that she did, indeed, keep her promise. You will also come to understand, as have I, that timelines are the multiple realities that exist parallel to this 3D reality in which humans on earth exist. As The Veil thins, and it is doing exactly that, more and more humans are awakening/learning/seeing/experiencing the same miracles/paranormal situations that I did as well as the other contributors to this book.

As we pass through 2024, there are those already living in 2025. Some live in a 5D reality. Some move back and forth between dimensions. Some "disappear" through portals (as seen on videos you can witness on YouTube and other venues), never to be seen in our reality. "Jumping" from one space to another, a la Star Trek is not fiction, as some would have you believe. My contributors, those I interview and want to remain anonymous, explain these experiences.

It is possible for us to create through our positive thoughts, visions, meditations, and focused intentions to create our reality. The world we all want is one of peace, joy, and harmony. When we read, hear, or even experience these angelic or divine interventions, do not dismiss them out of hand.

Do not think with the mind that is filled with fear and doubt.

Use your heart. Science has proven (Heart Math) that the heart has more "thinking-creative" ability than the mind. Your heart is where there is love. Love is the most powerful force and energy in the Universe.

Each time you have a CHOICE, stop.

"Choose wisely," as the Templar Knight said to Indiana Jones.

Make positive, honorable, loving choices in all matters.

These are the guiding words from your angels.

Two

WHERE DID THEY GO?

Never saw an angel? Are you so sure? And what if you did? Did you let the moment pass you by? Did you scratch your head at the time? Do you still wonder? If you are still in doubt and especially if you have not forgotten the incident, most likely that was an angel come to help you. There is a resonance to any angelic visit or contact with divine spirit that leaves an indelible memory in our psyche like no other experience. It is a reverberation in the heart that keeps that knowing pinging so that whenever we have another encounter with an angel, or feel the presence of the divine, though we cannot see them or hear them, we sense them and that is when we experience goosebumps, or hairs raising on the arms. Some call it a "spidey" sense. Antenna or just intuition. It is all these and more because we never forget a single detail and upon recall. It is as if the intervention happened only moments ago.

Again, I want to reiterate that I am not, nor have I ever claimed to be a theologian, pastor, or religious teacher. Nor do I want to be. I do not pass judgement on these stories. That is not the job I was given through my father during his NDE and the Being of Light. (That story is featured in ANGEL WATCH).

I am the chronicler.

My next stories are just a few, but they need to be shared.

This chapter deals with angels, sometimes who appeared as humans and then vanished into thin air. Some appeared as angels with wings.

They are here. They ARE with you.

BEGGAR OR ANGEL?

Angels that come to us disguised as human beings and then vanish into thin air have always been a source of fascination to me. Perhaps of all the stories I hear from others and the nearly incomprehensible experiences I have been the subject of, nothing makes my jaw drop as fast as a spine-tingly story about the angel who was there one minute and gone the next.

The very first time I think I ever heard this kind of story was while I was living in Houston many years ago. The woman who told me the story was somewhat of a flibberti-gibbet, my mother would have called her. She was theatrical and giddy and fun and overblown from her scarlet red lips to her pointy toed cowboy boots. I did not believe her when she said she had met an angel. I did not believe her as she told me the story about a stranger who had knocked on her door and begged for food.

Who does that kind of thing these days? I questioned.

If she were telling the story about someone during the Great Depression, sure, I would have gone along with that. My grandmother used to give food to "hoboes" she called them. She used to make soup on the weekends to hand out to needy people who came to her door on Sunday afternoons. It was her Christian duty.

However, in 1985 Houston, the town was awash in cowboy bars, oil money, a building boom, and most employers were begging people to come to work for them. Beggars did not come to the door and ask for food. Anyone coming to the door should have been regarded with a great deal of suspicion.

My dramatically dressed friend with her lime green cowboy hat with ostrich feathers poking out of the hat band, told me that she invited the beggar in. She gave him some Texas chili, cornbread, and sweet tea she had made. They had conversations about the weather. She repeatedly asked the stranger where he was from and he never gave her a straight answer. She asked him what kind of work he wanted. Maybe she could help him find something. He never answered her.

Finally, when he finished the meal, he thanked her and walked to the door. She opened it.

He walked out and then turned around.

She said at that moment, his eyes were sparkling blue, clear and riveting. "For I was hungry and you gave me to eat. Thank you, ma'am."

She stood in the doorway covered with chills as he walked a few steps down her sidewalk and onto the driveway. In front of her eyes, though the evening light was low, the man vanished in front of her very eyes. She rushed out of the house and looked everywhere. He was gone.

The woman told me that she knew she had been visited by an angel.

That was many years ago when I was told this story and as I write it now, I am blanketed with spiritual goosebumps. I am not afraid.

And I know I was the fool.

I did not believe her because she dressed so flamboyantly and appeared to be a ditsy woman. The woman was a devout Christian and helped her little church tremendously. She prayed every day and with all the scatter-brained ideas she came up with to make a living, she always, always believed that God would provide for her. She knew in her heart she was a blessed person.

And she was right.

The Lord had chosen her to experience this divine visit. All these years later, her story is the one that my mind will not release. It has haunted me all this time and is more real to me today than it was then when she told it to me. I do not know where this woman is today or even if she is alive. But wherever she is, she is protected, guided, and loved by the angels.

ANGEL ARTIST, ANGEL DEAR

Donna Voll is one of the most spiritually awake, aware, and angelically guided people I know. I have had the honor and pleasure to visit with her on her radio show, "Spirit Connections." You can reach Donna at www.angelstoguideyou.com.

It was Donna's own story that has moved me year in and year out when I talk to people about angels and their presence among us. I do not know why I should be so surprised by how much we humans must have more validation, and more evidence of the presence of the divine in our lives. Living on earth is so very, very difficult. Disease, heartbreak, financial ruin, pain, loss and just the shopping rage I feel standing in line at the monstrous super markets that have twenty-seven lanes available and only three people hired to check us out. All these things coupled with computers and cell phones that crash with all our essential personal contact information; our calendars and reminders; clogged traffic; bank errors; processed food that is filled with ingredients and preservatives guaranteed to create cancer, heart disease, warts and psoriasis are all enough reasons to want to run, hair-on-fire, right off the edge of a cliff. It is our belief that there is Someone, out there…God, who loves us and feels our pain. So, we trudge back to our mini-dwellings, take a deep breath and hope that tomorrow will be better.

Donna's personal story is that kind of story that has given me strength during the loss of my dearest loved ones; during frustrating days when "tossing the towel at someone" was more appropriate than "tossing in the towel."

Donna was twenty-eight years old when she met an angel in the flesh and he changed her life. Drastically.

Donna was working at a Metaphysical store behind the cash register one Saturday afternoon around five-twenty when "he" walked in.

He was tall and movie-star handsome with dark brown hair and blue eyes to rival the ocean on a brilliant sunny day. His energy was strong and male.

Donna started to shake before he said the first word. She knew something was very different. It was as if his energy reached out and grabbed her. She felt a vibration in her body that was not her imagination. It was very real.

She felt everything shifting inside her as if her very cell structure was being re-arranged. But by what?

The man was looking at her, holding her in a "place" and moment with his eyes. The moment was "profound." Donna had a clear knowing, an understanding that she was seeing the true form of this person. His energy was mesmerizing and compelling. She felt time stand still yet somehow, she was able to pull her eyes away from him in the hopes of re-gaining her bearings and her wits.

Donna was an artist but at this time in her life, she was at a crossroads. She did not feel she was advancing in her work. She loved painting portraits and discovered worlds within worlds when she peered into a person's face. But something in her heart told her that she could do more. Go deeper. She wanted to paint the soul, but she did not know how.

All her life, Donna had been clairvoyant and she saw angels even as a child. She saw "beings." They contacted her and she communicated with them. However, by the time she was in her twenties, she wanted to get it under control. She had started to pray and learned to meditate.

Her painting and her prayers were intertwined somehow, but they had not completely "jelled" the way she absolutely knew they should. Deep down she was convinced she had an amazing capacity of untapped talent that needed to be unlocked.

Also at this time, Donna had a friend who kept pushing her to get involved with the extra-terrestrial world. Something about aliens and their pursuits felt entirely wrong for Donna. The more her friend pushed her, the more she tried to break away from her friend. Talking to angels was second nature to Donna. Here, in their realm, she was free, loved, and comfortable. But the un-seen dimension of aliens was wrong for Donna. She felt a magnetism toward them and all the while she wondered if she was doing the right thing or the wrong thing.

It was at this life cross-road that Donna was visited by the handsome angel.

He was looking just past Donna now, to the area behind the counter where a row of her portraits was lined up, ready for pick-up from the owners. "I see that you are doing incredible art. What do you draw?"

She glanced at the portraits. "How do you know they're mine?"

"I know."

Donna felt a chill but she was not afraid. She faced him. "I do not draw. God draws," she said honestly. "They come from the spirit world," she continued feeling a rush of pride and honor.

"The alien world makes you uncomfortable."

"Yes. I am not going to deal with extraterrestrials."

"Then you couldn't draw any of your brothers or sisters that died, then, could you?"

"I don't know," Donna replied thinking that surely this man would transfigure into another being. He had waves of energy around him. There were no wings. He was bone and muscle and sinew.

"You know. Let's pray on that. I want you to understand today that angels are extraterrestrials. They are not human. Not in any way."

Then he started shaking.

He turned and walked out.

Donna was compelled to run after him. She rushed out the front door, reaching the sidewalk only seconds after he exited the shop.

He had vanished from sight. Donna looked up the sidewalk and down the street. Across the street. She wandered a few steps down the sidewalk and still did not find him.

"How is that possible?" Suddenly, she remembered that all things are possible with God.

"He WAS an angel!" Donna clamped her hands to her cheeks making sure she was still on earth herself. She walked back inside and remarked to herself that the angel had picked up things on her counter. He had thumbed through a book. He had touched a pen she had placed near the register. He had looked at it and then put it down. He was very, very real, indeed.

"He was manifested in the physical," she whispered to herself as awe filled her mind.

For days and weeks following the event, Donna prayed about her visitation. She wondered if she was to abandon the realm of discarnate beings who had befriended her and who communicated with her. She was not sure if she was to work more with them or less. She found it eerie, thought-provoking, and disturbing that all of this happened at the same time she was wallowing in consternation about her friend who believed in UFO's and aliens.

But for Donna, she prayed and what came to her was that she was aligned with the angels and that she had been chosen to work for them.

Shortly after that, her first "angel portrait" came through. It was in charcoal at first. What happened was that instead of drawing the human being, she saw the person's guardian angel/spiritual guide. Later, she began using colored chalks and brought the portraits to ethereal light. As time passed and Donna drew more portraits, at the bottom of the paintings were etchings of dead relatives, pets, guides, or other angels. Sometimes words in Hebrew came through. Donna would never know what was going to happen when she went to her easel.

Even to this day, Donna says that she can still feel the energy and the power that came off the angel that day. He changed her life and her career forever. He showed her the Way, the Path of Light and she had the courage to take it.

Donna states that the energy of Michael the Archangel comes through to her quite often.

I have been privileged to have one of Donna's portraits. It is not just beautiful but shockingly accurate. It is done in lavender chalk and the blonde angel has lavender eyes. She has a heart shaped face. There are two dogs, and yes, I had two dogs that died, Beau and Bebe. But what caused my chills were the sketches of a cat and Donna had named the kitten "Cat," which was the name of my first cat when I was a child. I also had two cats, Cinnamon, and Spice, who died within a month of each other in the late 1980's. There were several portraits of men all around me, that looked like my deceased father, uncles, and friends. There was even one of a small boy. I had a son who died at birth and many clairvoyants and mediums have told me that I have a young boy around me all the time.

Today, I look at the portrait and I find my newest shock. At the top right-hand corner of the portrait is a white butterfly. When my sister, Nancy, was dying in the hospital, one of the nurses, who also had cared for my father when he died, came into the room while Nancy was still conscious and said, "You know what you are, Nancy? You are a butterfly. A beautiful, colorful, huge butterfly. You are about to fly off to new adventures and a new life and you will be happy there."

Two days after Nancy died, my husband and I were sitting on the patio of our house looking at the pink blossoms of the redbud and crab apple trees, taking a quiet moment between all the preparations for Nancy's funeral. We saw a huge yellow butterfly dart from the maple trees, swoop down by us and go back to the Red Maple. My husband said, "It's Nancy."

"It is Nancy," I said.

A week later, I was back at work and Cheryl, our office manager, turned to me and said, "Nancy came to me in a dream last night and she asked me to ask you, 'Have you seen your first butterfly of the summer yet?'"

I started crying and said, "I did."

"That was Nancy."

I look at Donna's portrait of my guardian angel, whose name is Shariah, and I see the butterfly and I know that now years ago when Donna painted this portrait for me, she was being guided even more than SHE could imagine.

The butterfly is my symbol for Nancy's beautiful spirit. She was with me always when she was alive and she is with me always even in death.

Thank you, Donna, for sharing your wonderful story.

THE DARK NIGHT AND ANGEL GABRIEL

Author'S Note: *Suzanne's Story Written by Emil Toth*

Emil Toth is a talented author friend of mine who has written two books, *Patu* and *Seven Souls Before the Cross*. I have met Suzanne and she is a delightful soul. I always find it amazing when I meet the people who have gone through just such a trial and miracle such as this one with Suzanne. Thank you to Emil for writing the story and our deep gratitude to Suzanne for sharing one of the most haunting angelic stories I have ever heard.

*I*t all started the summer of my fourteenth birthday. I attended a bonfire with a friend and when we drove up, we were met by the guy throwing the party and a friend of his named David. David grabbed my hand and looked deeply in my eyes and said, "I'm going to marry you!" He was so sincere; it was love at first sight. We started dating and were inseparable.

He was shy and a nice guy. We took things slow at first but about three months later, we decided to have sex. It was the first time for both of us and it was awkward. As fate would have it, I got pregnant. Yes, you can get pregnant the first time.

Initially, I was very scared, knowing that only one other girl in our high school had gotten pregnant and she was shunned for the next three years. The truth was that I was not very popular. If fact, I was associated with a group called the "nerd herd." It was hard enough to take the mocking and insults from nearly everyone else in school as it was. I certainly did not want to be a total outcast.

However, as the shock about the pregnancy lessened, we both knew that our love was strong and that we wanted to have the baby and be a family. We knew it would be difficult, but we both came from good families and were sort of sure they would help us.

So, we waited until the start of the third trimester to tell our parents, just in case things did not go quite the way we thought they should. Abortion was illegal after the second trimester. My biggest fear was that my parents would force me to abort my baby. By waiting until after the second trimester, I reasoned that I was taking that option off the table. At least I thought I was.

That six months period was the strangest and most terrifying time for me. I was fearful someone would discover my pregnancy and at the same time, I was marveling at the life growing inside of me. Thank goodness it was in the 70's when hip-hugger jeans and peasant tops were the fashion. Peasant tops made everyone look pregnant. I could not believe my parents did not notice, but they did not.

Finally, the time did come when David and I had to tell our parents the truth. We started with David's father because he was the gentlest of all our parents. It was heartbreaking to watch him learn this news. I saw the hopes and dreams he had for David disintegrate in his eyes. His disappointment was more than we could bear. Somehow, we endured the first ordeal. Then it was time to tell David's mother.

In no way were we prepared for the violence of her reaction. She called me every nasty name in the book and blamed me for ruining her family. I was devastated. She called my parents to come over and while we waited, she continued to blast me with even more vile comments. My parents arrived and I was relieved until I had to watch the same reaction on their faces. Never had I disappointed my parents. I was a straight A student, very responsible, very gentle and I had destroyed my parents. I knew it would be bad, but never did I think it would be this sad.

The entire time I was carrying this child, I felt incredibly connected to God. God entrusted me with this new life and I loved him with all my heart. God needed me to bring this life into the world. I truly felt one with God helping Him in this act of creation. I had a wonderful peaceful knowingness that God would see us through this. Somehow, in His divine wisdom He would help our parents realize that this was not the end of the world.

David's father was a doctor. He made a few phone calls and found a doctor friend of his who would lie about the gestation of the baby. He agreed to perform the abortion.

I was shocked.

David and I pleaded with his family and mine, but to no avail. Both of our parents were determined not to allow the birth of this child, not even to give it up for adoption (which I am sure would have been beyond traumatic). They were sure that a child born to two children would be impossible, knowing that they would have to help raise it. College was a must for both of us and there just was not room for a baby in their eyes. They told us that they were saving us from ourselves.

My parents literally packed me up and took me to a women's hospital in Michigan. It was there that they would kill the very life within me. I felt as if I were being taken to the gallows. I was numb knowing that I was ending the life of my baby, but both the baby and I were helpless to stop the madness.

David was not allowed to be with me, so he stayed at the hotel with my mom. I had to do this alone.

At the hospital, I was hooked up to an IV drip in my wrist and a tube was inserted in my tummy. Saline was pumped into my stomach to kill my baby. Since I was so far along, I would have to deliver my dead baby. I never felt so alone and the realization that I had disappointed God, was more than I could handle.

Delivery did not come quickly or easily. My body was wracked with pains that I had to suffer through for long torturous hours. Nurses and my doctor came and went all night checking on my progress. My tears were endless. I felt like a monster. I wanted to die!

During all this insanity, a very gentle man, an intern named Gabriel, came to check on me. He decided he would stay with me and help me through the night. Even as the nurses came and went, Gabriel remained by my side. When we were alone, we would talk. His voice was very soothing and calming. His words encouraging. Eventually, I relaxed. He held my hand through the pains. Gabriel listened to my sorrow, wiped away my tears, and was patient as I lamented my loss. Gabriel assured me that God loved me more than ever and told me how brave I was being. He told me that God knew how much I loved the baby and what I had endured in my efforts to keep my baby. God was proud of me, he said. Together, Gabriel and I made it through the night.

By daybreak, the baby was coming and my little boy was delivered. His dead, lifeless body was put in a pan and taken from the room. A part of me died that day and if it was not for Gabriel, I would not have lived through the emotional pain. His assurance that God still loved me made all the difference to my sanity and my soul.

I carry sadness from this but no guilt or shame. I was and am eternally grateful to Gabriel.

When I was leaving the hospital, I wanted to say good-bye and thank-you to Gabriel. I stopped at the front desk and asked for him. The nurse looked at me like I was nuts. Another nurse asked who I was talking about. I told her I wanted to thank Gabriel for being with me all night. This nurse looked more confused than the first nurse.

They told me in no uncertain terms that no one named Gabriel worked at the hospital. There was no doctor, nurse, nurse's aide or even an orderly with the name of Gabriel

Then, they told me that I must have been hallucinating because no one sat with me all night. I was alone in my room. They told me that they had come and gone from my room, but no one had been with me.

I knew then that God loved me so much that even when I was killing His creation, He wanted me to know that He loved me! Gabriel has been a part of my life since then, but never as strong a presence as he was that dark and horrible night. I was blessed by his presence during my most terrible moment and I am still truly blessed.

Three

ANGELS KNOW BARRIERS OR BOUNDARIES

Angels, the messengers from God/One Source, reveal themselves regardless of your religion, your social taboos, your sometimes arrogant mindset. If they think you need a swift kick of wisdom and truth, they will bring it on. If you are thinking these beings are passive, think again. They know when they are needed. They respond to our requests. You may think they do not act when you still have not suddenly discovered a brand-new car in your driveway or gotten a raise (when you did not ask for one). Though I will tell you, I DO have stories from people who did mysteriously receive a new car when they desperately needed one. And many are the stories I have from others who lost their job through no fault of their own, only to land a better job that truly made them happy. Miracles do abound. I see them by the dozens every day. The following is one of my "miracle" stories that came back to me.

ANGEL IN PRISON

Author's Note: Again, my thanks to George Noory and the "Coast to Coast" radio program staff, where I have met so many wonderful people who are willing to share their amazing real-life stories with me.

This story was sent to me by Robert Borrego. This is one of a handful of angel stories that got lost several years ago when my web site crashed and I thought I had lost all these emails.

Miraculously, and I do not say that facetiously, either, because the event of all these stories coming back to me when I need them, is more than a divine nudge. It is a real angel "pelting." How awesome is our generous and spirit-filled Universe that things like this usually do happen for a reason. It may take us years and years, even decades to know the reason, but there is always a reason.

The following is a story of a real angel sighting.

Back in the 1980's and 1990's I was a correctional officer for the California Youth Authority. I worked the graveyard shift and was the only officer in charge of a unit containing ninety to ninety-five wards. Typically, it would be quite noisy until about midnight. By around three in the morning, I would have trouble staying awake.

One early morning I was resting in the back office and had closed my eyes for a moment only to fall asleep.

This, of course, was incredibly frowned upon by my superiors. There was always the potential danger that one of the inmates would sometimes escape from their rooms.

This fact always stays in my consciousness and so, even when I doze, it is not for long.

Slowly I awoke and the minute that I did, I felt a presence. I knew I was not alone in that room. Every hair on my arms and the back of my neck stood on end. I could feel the adrenaline in my body kick into high gear.

Because I knew the precarious nature of my business, I was fully prepared to come face to face with an inmate, bowed over me and ready to pounce. But as I opened my eyes and scanned the room, I held my breath. I was all too aware that I could be in for the fight of my life. I certainly would not have been the first staff member to have been murdered at the Youth Authority. Every correctional officer knew the truth about the Youth Authority. We dealt with felons, not juvenile delinquents.

I moved only my eyes from left to right. I kept my head still so that my predator might not realize I was fully awake.

My eyes stopped cold. My breath froze in my lungs as I gasped. Standing off to my right was the most glorious being I have ever seen.

"Angel," was all I could say.

He, and I say that because he looked like a male, was about six feet plus tall. He wore a white robe that fell to the floor. But it was his magnificent white wings that held me spellbound. They, too, reached the floor. They were mighty and strong and so very white! His brown hair was shoulder length.

He did not say anything and I do not remember if he even smiled at me. But somehow, I knew it was important at this moment that he was showing himself to me.

I had a pervasive sense that he was there to protect me. Not just protect me in my work, but to always be there for me.

At that moment I remembered thinking that when I was young and Catholic, I wanted to be a priest. I suppose all Catholic altar boys want to be a priest at one time or another. I had not thought much about those days but with an angel standing in the room with me, I did think about it.

I believe that he was and is my guardian angel.

I looked away for just a moment scanning the rest of the room, because I was wide awake and I was supposed to be on duty. When I looked back, the angel had disappeared.

I do not think he went away. I think he is still with me. It was just that at that moment in time and space, our two dimensions/worlds had been open to each other.

I had my moment of divine connection and it was amazing.

All I can say is, I sure hope I see him again someday!

ANGEL IN THE SNOWSTORM

Author Note: This is one of my personal angelic interventions.

It does not matter how young or old we are, divine aide and support are always with us. God loves us and sends angels to keep reminding us how much.

During the time that my parents were building the house they were to live in for the rest of their lives, we lived in a little rent cottage at Fish Lake, Indiana. I was only two years old and had just turned three when my mother, who was pregnant with twins, started hemorrhaging. My brother, Ed, was a year younger than I was, so my mother had her hands full with two toddlers and an advanced pregnancy.

It was February and a snow storm had just blown in. Our rental cottage was meant for summertime visitors and probably built for short-time visitors. The walls were paper thin and there was no such thing as insulation or much heat from a very small coal furnace. My mother used to talk about the winter there when there was ice on the inside walls six inches thick. She used to put our snowsuits, mittens, hats, and triple socks on us when she put us down to bed at night.

I always thought these stories were exaggerated until I asked my father and he confirmed it. He said that in 1949, there was very little in the way of housing materials, which made it difficult to build our "new" house. The summer cottage was all that was available to rent in those days after the World War II.

The heat-less and faulty-lock infested rental cottage was not equipped for a human dwelling as should be apparent by now. Therefore, the fact that this cottage did not have a telephone will be no surprise. Since heat was not a high priority, a telephone would be very far down on the list.

On this snowing February day, my mother was going down to the basement and had been carrying me in her right arm and my baby brother, Ed, in her left arm. She tripped and all three of us fell down the stairs.

Blessedly, neither myself or my brother were hurt. My mother was a different story. Within minutes of getting us up the stairs she started having pains in her stomach. Then the hemorrhaging started.

There was no phone. It was the dead of winter and there were no winter residents or neighbors around. This was a summer place. There was only a little grocery store about two blocks away at the end of our road. There was a telephone at the grocery store.

My mother bundled me up in my snowsuit, hat, mittens, and boots. She tied a scarf around my mouth and nose so that only my eyes were exposed to the cold. She gave me a note to give to the man who owned the grocery store. The note informed him that she was pregnant and bleeding and to call an ambulance. She wrote the address down.

She put the note inside my mitten.

"Cathy, keep this note tight in your hand. Tell the man to send an ambulance. Just go to the end of our road. You remember where the grocery is. We were just there yesterday. Hurry as fast as you can."

I walked out the front door and started walking.

The snow, which had looked pretty from inside my bedroom, was now a thick white curtain. The wind was blowing at what to a three-year-old child must have seemed like gale force winds. The snow got deeper, but I kept walking.

I could not see a thing. Everything was white. The buildings were white, the trees were white, the road was white. I could not discern anything. The grocery had an advertisement for Kreamo bread with a little girl painted on the outside brick wall. All I knew was that I had to find that grocery so that my mother could get to a doctor. I was very scared being alone, but there was no one else to help my mother but me.

I kept walking. And walking.

The blizzard was one of the worst that had hit our area in years. I walked for what seemed a very long time to me.

Over a mile from our rental cottage was a bridge. (As I remember.) Seeing the bridge, I now knew I was a long way from the grocery.

Out of the whirl of snow and wind, a pair of headlights seared through the distance. The car crept toward me. The driver, undoubtedly could not see any better than I could.

It stopped right beside me. The driver got out of the car and came over to me. I stood stock still. This was a stranger and he was talking to me.

"Little person, what are you doing out in this storm?"

"I have to go the grocery store."

"All by yourself?"

"I have to get the man there to call an ambulance for my mother. I have a note."

"Can I see it?" Since this man was a stranger and I was more terrified of talking to a stranger than dying in a snowstorm, I said, "No. It's for the man at the grocery store."

"You are a long way from the store, but I know where it is. I will drive you there."

"I'm not supposed to get into the car with strangers."

"I will not hurt you. I promise. But we must get help for your mother. You would not want anything bad to happen to her, would you?"

"No," I replied looking from him to his car with the headlights illuminating the giant snowflakes.

"Please, let me help you," he said and opened the car door for me.

He tugged on my mitten covered hand. "Please we must hurry to help your mother. I do not know what happened but it had to be awful for her to send her little girl out in a blizzard to get help."

I started to cry. "I have to help her."

I got in the car and the stranger closed the door. I will never forget sitting in that car, hanging onto the door handle with both hands. Just in case he tried to kill me or eat me, I had heard those stories, too, from the babysitters who read to me out of fairy tale books, I figured I could open the door and jump out. I remember the inside of the car was grey. There was grey fabric on the car door interior walls and the seats were grey. But it was warm inside the car.

It seemed like forever, but he did drive me to the grocery store. Only when I was inside and saw the familiar face of the man who owned the grocery store, did I take out my precious note and hand it to him.

"Good God in heaven!" The grocery store owner immediately called for the ambulance. He told the stranger that he would drive me to my house since he knew where I lived.

The stranger walked out of the grocery store and drove away.

By the time I got home with the grocery store owner, my mother was in terrible pain. It was not long after that that the ambulance arrived. The grocery store owner had called my father at his office and he made certain a lady who lived at a nearby farm came to get my brother and myself. My father met the ambulance at the hospital when my mother was brought in.

I never forgot any of this, but aspects of it were unclear in my mind for a long time. About a decade or more ago, I asked my mother if she ever knew who the stranger was who picked me up.

"Why no. None of us had ever seen him before. The man who owned the grocery store did not know him. He did not leave a name either, so that we could thank him. We have always thought it rather eerie. Fish Lake was nearly abandoned in the winter in those days. Few people lived out our way and those who did live there or even rent their houses out were known, certainly, by the man at the grocery store. It is unlikely that on that day and in that blizzard that anyone would be out sightseeing. I suppose there is a rational explanation for his presence, but I have never come up with one."

"How would you explain it, Mom?"

"I have always believed he was an angel."

In these contemporary times young mothers would not dream of ever sending a three-year-old out into a snowstorm to walk even that couple blocks. Young mothers now do not even let their children play outside in their own yards without supervision. They watch their kids like hawks. I am not sure if that is a good thing or a bad thing.

I cannot imagine how terrified my mother must have been when the blizzard raged and got worse and worse. She had no phone, no pager to call me. I was gone a long time. She was in horrid pain and was losing blood by the pint. And she had another baby at home. Frightening times.

My twin sisters did not live. My mother struggled to save them, but God had other plans. Sharon Lynn and Theresa Louise were their names.

I always wonder what would have happened if the stranger had not come by when he did. I would have kept walking in the snowstorm. It was so blinding someone could have run over me. I might have frozen to death. If no one had come for my mother, she probably would have died as well.

Life is full of possibilities and precarious twists and spins of fate. It is even more reason to be grateful and thankful for the very minutes in which we live and where we have one more chance to love.

Four

VANISHING MEDICAL ANGELS

When you read the following story, or others like it in my book, *Angel Watch* about Medical Teams and healers who move through the dimensions from The Other Side to this 3D realm, I hope you burn these stories into your mind and heart. Then imagine, if you will, a world, a new timeline, where there is no disease, no pain or suffering. What if angels or multi-dimensional beings came to us as an everyday occurrence and healed us?

On November 19, 2024 I fell in my garage on the cement floor and shattered my left radius and ulna. I broke my right radius. Yes. Both arms. I will skip the details, aside to say that from the get-go, I had angelic help.

As I was falling, I literally heard a voice say, "Don't hit your head. Don't hit your head." Just as I made contact with the cement, I turned my head slightly to the left, where if I would have hit it, I would have smacked my temple on the cement. Would I have died? Possible. But instead, I hit my chin. I thought to myself, "Don't hit your chin."

Then I distinctly felt something, someone? Pull my hair so that my chin did not hit a second time where I could have broken my jaw. My teeth. Broken my palate? Who knows? But something stopped that from happening.

Shock and pain ensued. I felt my left arm and knew the bones were a mess. I tried to straighten them out. I had no phone with me. I was alone as Bill was at the store. My neighbor came home and I shouted for him, but he could barely hear me. Now, I was trying to cry loud enough through the pain, Bill drove home. He had come back early because he had forgotten his wallet. (Another angelic move.)

Once I was in the hospital and X-rays taken, Bill called the orthopedic surgeon whom I was to see in the morning and who was a friend of Bill's. Scott was incredible. He immediately went on line, saw my X-rays, and suggested I see an orthopedic surgeon he knew who dealt with shattered bones. The next morning, I was in that surgeon's office. The following morning, I was in surgery. A week later I had surgery on my right arm.

Yes. I did not die. That was miracle enough. But here is the angelic healing story.

After the second surgery and the nerve block had painfully worn off, I had a dream.

I saw thousands of angels gathering outside my house on the golf course and floating toward my house. As they came closer, a group of four or five of these angels, all in dazzling white long tunics, walked into the house through the front door. There were two extra tall glowing white beings, who came down the hall first. There were two more behind them, though not as tall. All four came into my bedroom and stood at the end of my bed.

I asked them their purpose.

"We are here to help heal you," the one standing closest to the door said to me telepathically.

I sat up in the bed and presented my casted left arm. In the dream---or was it a dream? The cast fell away. The Being took my arm into his hands and kept running his hands up and down my arm. I saw colored lights emanate from his hands. I remember seeing a lot of purple and gold. When I think back to these beings, they did not have wings. Their arms and hands were quite thin and the fingers were longer.

I do not believe they were angels. I believe they were multi-dimensional Light Beings. Extra-terrestrials. They did not say who they were or where they were from. But they were loving and focused on the work they were there to perform.

The following week, I went back to the doctor's therapy unit. The therapist was more than a little surprised at my progress. I am not a young kid. I have osteoporosis. The surgeon said that my shattered bones were one of the five worst cases he had performed in all his years of practice. Yet, I was healing like an athlete.

We have a friend who is not only a psychic medium, but is very connected to angels. When I asked her about my fall, I told her that I was told by my own angels that the angels and Jesus were there that day to save me. She confirmed this as truth.

I am writing this book in and out of my breakaway casts. I can type till the pain is too much.

The angels want you to know these stories.

Here is another.

ANGELS TO HEAL MY SON

Author's Note: This story was sent to me by Jim Shannon. It is a startling and dramatic story of angels coming to the rescue. As a parent, I cannot imagine Jim's terror during this time and his awe over what happened when two angels came to heal his son.

As I sit here typing this letter out, I look over at my 18-year-old son as he lays on the couch sleeping after just having surgery to repair his ACL. I am still asking God for an answer as to why this happened to him. It is not a terrible surgery but it is what was lost when he did this.

My son is a senior this year and this was his year to shine in basketball. He has worked hard to be the great player he is. His team was counting on him and we looked forward to watching him play his final high school games.

There were a lot of scouts looking at him. In December 22, 2011 in front of a full house, my son went down after tearing his ACL. The place became silent as they carried my son off the court. He rehabbed for a month hoping to come back and during his first game back within one minute he went down again.

He texted me from the locker room and told us how lucky he was to have us as parents, but then told my wife and I that this would be the last time he would put on a high school uniform.

That is not the story. Not the real story.

All this time I have been questioning God, as to why this had to happen. I understand things could be worse and I do not see the big picture as to why, but all right then, here is my angel story and this is why I should not question God.

It was a warm summer afternoon when my son, Jarrett, and I went down to play some basketball at the YMCA. Jarrett was a little kid in 3rd grade who weighed about 85 pounds but had the heart and skills of a kid twice his age. He was not afraid to go against anyone in a basketball game.

Jarrett was always saying, "Dad, let's go over and play those kids," knowing quite well they were college kids. Jarrett did not care. He was up for the challenge. Everyone was always amazed at how well he played.

We ended up playing three on three against these kids that were out of high school. The kid who guarded me was a big boy weighing easily 250 pounds. The boy guarding Jarrett was thin and very surprised at how well my son played.

We would check the ball in and Jarrett would go to his left each time and score on his player. The guy who was guarding me kept yelling at his player to guard my son to his left but he could not do it.

Jarrett kept scoring.

The next time Jarrett got the ball, my guard ran after Jarrett to block his shot, and when he did, he accidentally knocked Jarrett down to the floor and all 250 pounds of this big boy fell and landed right on top of my eighty-five-pound son.

It all happened in slow motion.

Jarrett instantly screamed in pain. I ran over and knelt by his side. I thought he was going to die. He looked like he was starting to go into convolutions and was trying to catch his breath. I knew he was in shock.

He kept telling me, "Dad my arm! My arm hurts so bad!" He was stuttering and could barely catch his breath to talk.

I tried to calm him down and as I looked up at the guy who landed on him, there were tears running down his cheeks. "I'm sorry. I'm so sorry."

What you must know is that Jarrett and I go to the Y a lot and we pretty much know everyone there. You can always tell the newbies and the strangers when they show up.

As I was kneeling in front of Jarrett, trying to comfort him these two ladies approached from apparently out of nowhere. One of them tapped me on my shoulder and said, "Sir, could you please move and let me take a look at him?"

Both these ladies wore dark glasses and one of them had a scarf on her head. I thought that she looked too young to be wearing one of those things on her head.

The one with the scarf was the observer. She just stood there watching and guarding while the other lady tended to my son.

As she talked to Jarrett, she placed her hand over his chest and said, "Son, I need you to slow your breathing down."

Then she ran her hand from one side of his chest to the other. As she did this, his breathing slowed to normal, not in a few minutes but right there, right then.

As she was doing this, Jarrett was crying and said, "I think my arm is broken."

She picked his arm up and as he described to me later, she ran both her hands down his arm. Jarrett said it felt like how your arm feels when it falls asleep as if little jolts of electricity or needles were pricking him.

This was the same sensation he felt when she touched his chest.

Everyone just stood there as if time had slowed down. This all happened within maybe three minutes.

As he stopped crying, she got closer to his face and said, "Now, get up."

I was thinking, Oh, my God! No!

I knew it was always dangerous to move an accident victim. It was doubly dangerous for Jarrett, especially after seeing my son get squashed by this big kid. This kid landed so hard on my son that he bounced up after hitting him and landed on him again.

There was no way Jarrett should be getting up.

The woman got a little closer to his ear and said, "Get up."

He slowly got up and she told him to go over and get a drink of water.

We walked over and got a drink of water and as I turned around, they were gone. They had vanished. I looked at the doorways and exits. Gone. Poof. GONE!

Though I was stunned, I looked at Jarrett and was so thankful he was alive. "Let's go home."

As he wiped off the remaining tears he said, "Dad, I'm okay. Let's go finish the game."

I thought he was crazy, but Jarrett insisted.

And we did finish the game.

As I sit here again watching him sleep after surgery, after missing out on his senior year and after typing this letter, I must think that God is watching out for him. His direction in life will now take on a route that God wants him to go. I must believe that.

Thank you, Catherine, for letting me share my story.

Five

VISITATIONS FROM DEPARTED LOVED ONES

Author Note: Celestial guidance is not confined only to Angels and Archangels.

Many of our departed family and friends continue to show their love and concern for us after their death. Leaving the body is not the end of life. We are spiritual, energy beings who take on matter in the form of a human body to learn and grow spiritually through the struggles, joys, loves and sorrows in this reality, or as some now call our 3D reality, this matrix or simulation. What matters here, is the LOVE that blasts through the Veil between the dimensions when our departed loved ones come to us in the daylight to aid us.

There are visitations from our departed loved ones that are meant to reassure us and ease our anguish and grief. For some of us these visitations are wisps of encounters that are so brief and even "disconnected" from what we are otherwise doing and thinking, that it is easy for us to explain them away until they disappear in our consciousness. We tell ourselves, "That didn't happen." We are quick to rationalize the shadow we see out of the corner of our eye at precisely the moment we were humming our departed mother's favorite song. How easy it is to continue putting the groceries away or working on the computer and not give that second of pause to remember our dead brother or sister and thank them for looking over our shoulder and helping us make it through another day.

How simple to brush away a memory of a lovely holiday dinner our departed best friend served to us. Or maybe you have a friend whom you wronged and you never had a chance to tell them that you were sorry. That apology is still possible. When the thought of that person or the vision of their face fleets across your mind, stop and talk to them. Say a little prayer for them. They will thank you by saying a prayer for you. They will return your kindness. And isn't that what Jesus said, that we will receive back what we give seven times seven? Even a thousand-fold? He went even further and told us that it was just as important to be merciful to our enemies. What greater gift is there than that? To allow your heart to be filled with so much compassion that you can pray for those who wronged you, is about as close as we can get to knowing the kind of mercy that God, Himself, has for you.

Most people believe that when you die, that everything ends. It is over. They also believe that for their loved one "they are in heaven" and as such, they have moved on. They have a new life and that they are no longer part of our lives.

The flip side of our technology-oriented world that we live in, is the fact that these same breakthroughs in medical science have given us the ability to bring people back from the brink of death. Years ago, when my father had his first of several near-death-experiences, these medical "rescues" were rare. These days there are millions of NDE's. They are no longer rare. Most of us are not quite so shocked, when we hear about people or even know a person who has literally died on a gurney or in the operating room and lived to talk about it.

Not all these people have a spiritual experience, either. But fortunately for those of us who are searching and eager to learn more about our life in the world to come, many of these people are bolstered by courage and probably a good dose of the Holy Spirit, to speak up and describe what it is like to die.

We are learning that life is hardly over when we die. Death on earth is truly our new birth in heaven.

As humans, we are so plugged-into our highly technical, science-oriented world that constantly validates *only* that which is considered as "normal," "real" and "acceptable." In this contemporary age of emphasis on all that is "politically correct" we are even more reluctant to tell others about the most important testimonies of our lives... our spiritual experiences.

In the past decade we have become even more "disconnected" from our feelings, emotions, and our spiritual needs than ever before. We "text" our family and friends even during meals when we are sitting with people we should be communicating with and listening to. We email our business associates. Seldom do we pick up a phone and talk to our agents, co-workers, clients, patients, and bosses. In a telephone call we can hear the emotions others are experiencing. We can hear frustration and pain. We can hear joy and enthusiasm. Most of us are not writers and do not know how to use words properly to express our deepest feelings or our most profound thoughts.

This electronic and byte-memory contemporary terrain we inhabit has inured us to the only experiences in life we were meant to live by our Creator…. those of the heart and soul.

It is no wonder we mock and disdain those who are open to angels and the Holy Spirit. We keep our own "selves" closed off to all that could possibly target us as "freaks." And yet, the creative side of our being is screaming to be heard every minute.

But are any of us listening?

Again, I applaud those of you who have come forward to bring your stories to the rest of us. I know that you are putting your reputation on the line for us. This sacrifice of yours is truly appreciated. Without you and your willingness to risk being labeled an outcast and as something abnormal, the rest of us might not find our way back to our Divine Path.

Bless you.

BROTHER ANGEL

Author's Note: This story was sent to me by Bob Zimmerman. In his email to me he said that only because he heard me on *Coast-to-Coast* radio show, did he have the courage to share this experience.

I don't blame him. As I said that night to George Noory. Only two times have I ever heard of instances in which a departed loved one comes back and can enter or take over our bodies. Only four days before my father's death he told me that at night there were spirits of people who had lived before that came to his bedroom and tried to enter his body. Some did take him over, but they immediately jumped back out. "They told me that my body was too decrepit," my father said.

The other instance is of my sister Nancy coming back to visit Lucy. Nancy did not take over Lucy's body, however, she stuck her hand inside Lucy's chest and held her heart. That is still is very unsettling to me.

I have always and will always keep my mind and heart and intentions on the positive things in life and after this life. I intentionally do not discuss the dark side, dark forces, or negative aspects of the world beyond the veil. Everyday life on the earth plane is difficult and frustrating enough without conjuring up negative thoughts.

This next story is quite thought-provoking. Bob's experience is a very positive one and gives him comfort and peace. That is the reason I asked him to share this story with us.

This happened several years ago. My older brother passed away one and half years earlier than this incident. By this time, I felt I had dealt with my grief and anguish over his death.

One night just as I got into bed, turned out the light and was settling in, I heard someone in the room call my name.

"Bob."

It did not hit me for a few seconds and I thought to myself, *Did I just hear my name called?*

As I was lying on my side, suddenly, I felt the hairs on my arms standing straight up. I was covered in chills. Then I felt something go through my arm.

I felt it come out of my arm. Then it entered my body lengthwise since I was lying on my side and go through me, and come out the other side as if was rolling right through me.

It was the coldest thing I have ever felt. During this experience, I must say that I was very calm; almost to the point of not being able to move.

When it was over, (I knew I was having an experience) instead of jumping up and turning on the lights, I just laid there relaxed. I eventually fell asleep.

When I finally told my wife a week later, she said, "That was your brother. He came to you. I believe that he needs your prayers."

As I looked at her, I realized that it was my brother's voice I had heard calling me. She was right. He had come to me for a reason.

That night, I prayed for him. I told him it was all right to go on. He did not have to stay here to protect me. I wanted him to be happy.

I also asked him to give me a sign that it was truly him who had come to me that night. If he could give me another sign, I would be very appreciative.

The very next night, I was sitting at my computer in my bedroom when I heard a popping sound in the hallway. Exactly when I looked up, I saw my brother walk by the open doorway. I had two seconds, and in those two seconds I saw so much. First, he was much younger—in his thirties. He looked so clean and fresh to me. Second, the hall was dark, but he was lit up in the brightest light I have ever seen-and it was not a glaring light. He was looking straight ahead and had a very relaxed, calm smile on his face. I got the impression he was walking towards someone who was waiting for him. And at the same time, I knew it was not really him, but his Angel. And then he was gone. He just vanished.

I searched the house and I was alone. Of course, I could not believe what just happened, but as I re-live this experience almost every day, I wonder why. Why choose me? Why was I allowed to experience this? I knew then I would never see him again.

I really think I saw him walking into Heaven. And I think, as my older brother, he was concerned about me, and wanted to let me know life goes on.

You see, we had a middle brother who took his own life, and I think he was concerned about that. I believe my brother's angel let him come to me.

Thank you, Angel.

GEORGIE'S GOODBYE

Author Note: The following story was sent to me by another talented author, Phyllis Uzelac, whom I have worked with now for years. She is not only a good friend, but a sister of the soul who understands the life in the world to come.

Pfc. George Stephen Straszewski of Gary, Indiana died November 30, 1968 from hostile kill in South Vietnam. Georgie was a Marine. He was eighteen years old.

The Straszewskis were our neighbors. Georgie spent a lot of time at our house. He was my brother, Mark's, best friend. They would most often be seen riding around the neighborhood on Mark's white motor scooter. Where you saw one, you could usually find the other.

Georgie was a friendly, cheerful young man. His smile was contagious and everyone enjoyed being around him. His parents were planning for him to go to college. His death was a tragic loss to many, especially his mother, father, and older brother.

My husband, Ted, returned from Viet Nam in April of nineteen sixty-eight. Georgie listened intently to Ted's stories about the war, the country, and the people he encountered during his tour as a combat medic in Viet Nam. It fascinated him. We did not realize at the time just how much of an impact Ted's experiences had on Georgie until he announced that he had enlisted in the marines. Ted's reaction was solemn. He failed to mention the nightmares he was having since his return home.

Georgie's parents were upset over their son's decision to join the service during a time of war. They came to America after World War II for the main purpose of raising their children in a free country where they would be safe from the casualties of war.

Mr. Zygmont Straszewski was a brilliant man. He had a Master's Degree in agriculture and a Masters in chemistry. He was captured and his intelligence utilized by the Germans during World War II where he was held in the prisoner of war camp, Murnau. Zygmont suffered the hardships of separation from his wife and the living conditions of being a prisoner of war. He once described a typical day as consisting of two meals, which were thinned soup and a sparsely cut slice of black bread. Between those meals were long hard hours of work and labor for the Germans who had captured him. He stated that only the strong of spirit, mind and body survived. The loss of his youngest son to hostile fire was more than he could bear.

My husband and I lived only a couple of miles from our old neighborhood. I have always been afraid of the dark. The sky was heavy with clouds that night making it seem darker than usual. I kept the shades opened and could usually see the moon through my bedroom window. But on this evening, on the last day of November, 1968, there was no moon to comfort me from the inky blackness of the night. I looked over at my husband, who was sleeping soundly and decided to get up and read the letter that I had just received that morning from Georgie.

This letter was different from his usual exciting, informative, messages where he would describe the jungle, his pride of being there, the bugs, snakes, and people. I felt his sadness as I read the dismal words he expressed and I realized that he was telling me good bye.

It was difficult reading about his fears and the dread that he could not share with his parents. Georgie knew that he was going to die.

As he described the mission that would be his last, he explained how he was going to have to walk point into enemy territory. Walking point meant that he had to assume the first and most exposed position in a combat military formation. He would be blindly walking into a massacre while leading the men in his unit through unsecured, hostile territory. Georgie would be the first one visible to hostile fire. They were aware that the area was full of Viet Cong and it would be a very dangerous mission in a prime killing zone. He then said that he knew he would not be making it out alive.

Periodically, I would have to stop reading, so that I could wipe the tears that were burning my eyes as Georgie poured his heart out to me in this horrendously emotional letter. Though I recognized his fear, I realized that he was more concerned about how his parents were going to handle his death and that he would never be able to say good bye to them. Georgie was saddened by the pain and anguish that his parents would suffer.

It was the last letter I ever received from Georgie. He asked me to please, comfort his parents and brother. He wrote that he realized that his father suffered at the hands of the Germans in World War II and did not want him to have to think about all of that when they were informed of his death.

At this point, I had to put the lengthy letter down as I realized that he would be walking in that position on that very day. He could be dead already for all I knew. I read the letter on November 30, 1968; the day Georgie was killed. My husband woke up to find me crying at the kitchen table over Georgie's letter. He tried to comfort me by telling me that every time a soldier goes into battle, he does not know if he'll live through it.

As I was explaining my emotional reaction to the letter to my husband, the telephone rang. I answered it quickly. It was my father. He told me that he was awakened from sleep by the sound of a big explosion followed by heavy marching boots of soldiers. It was coming from the attic above his bed. He and my brother Mark searched the cob web covered attic and found nothing. I shared the letter with my father and at that moment we both knew that Georgie had been killed.

It was close to a week after that horrible night of revelations that Georgie's dad called to tell me that a military car was in their drive way. They did not want to answer the door. I rushed over to their house and found three military men patiently waiting for the terrified couple that was huddled closely together in front of the window wearing terror-stricken expressions. When they saw me, they opened the front door.

I watched these two people, whom I respected and cared for, fall apart as one of the officers began to express his sympathy. Mr. Straszewski collapsed and landed on his hands and knees. His wife simply stared in shock, unable to deal with her own state of emotions. She could not even cry, but stood speechless as the young Marine official informed them of the news that Georgie was dead.

One of the military men moved robotically as he handed Renee an American flag and told them that they would be informed when the body would be returned to the states. At that time, they would receive Georgie's dog tags and personal effects.

Georgie's father looked up at the young Marine. His face was pale and the light had slipped away from his once twinkling eyes. He asked him how it happened. He wanted to know how his son died.

One of the other Marines spoke up. He told the heart sick parents that Georgie died a hero. He told them that their son was killed by a mortar during an attack in South Viet Nam as he walked point. I remember him then asking if there was anything that they could do for them. Mr. Straszewski asked, "Can you give my son back his life?"

The three Marines just lowered their heads and told him how sorry they were to have to report such horrible news.

Since that time, Georgie's father passed away. He was finally able to be reunited with his precious son. I speak to Renee frequently. She told me that Zygmont died from a broken heart. He never got over the loss.

Renee told me that she thinks about her son every day. The reason they moved out of their house in Gary was because she continued to see her son after the funeral. He walked the halls of their home at night. He called to her from his bedroom and when she would get up, he would be standing in the doorway holding his arms out to her.

There was one incredible incident that happened in broad daylight and which is nearly impossible for me to believe, even as I sit here writing it down.

Renee was sitting in her living room one day, when she heard the beeping sound of my brother's motor scooter. When she looked out of the window, she saw Mark drive up on his white motor scooter.

Riding behind Mark, was Georgie...in the flesh.

There was nothing transparent or ghost-like to Georgie's appearance. He was sitting behind his friend, Mark, just as he had always done.

Georgie waved to his mother with a big smile on his face. He was as carefree as anyone would have been on a beautiful day with the sun shining and life happening all around him.

Renee waved back to her son and felt a huge tug at her heart.

Like many of us who have such encounters, Renee continually espoused to me that she was not insane. She saw what she saw and what she saw was real.

It was as if Georgie had never died at all.

"I know my son's voice when I hear it. Every mother does."

Despite my efforts to always steer the conversation to other family members whenever I talk with Renee, she cannot let him go. Inevitably, we always end up talking about Georgie. His mother speaks hopefully of the day when they will all be together again.

I believe that Georgie is with his mother every day of her life here on earth. It would not surprise me a bit to get a phone call from her in which she tells me that she has seen Georgie again.

Like her, I look forward to that next time when Georgie comes to visit.

LUCY'S VISITATION FROM NANCY

My sister, Nancy, was very close to Lucy. In fact, they were as close as sisters could ever possibly be. As young mothers, they lived back door to back door and their kids were in and out of each other's houses all day. They worked on civic projects together and generally they saw eye to eye on nearly every subject imaginable. To say they loved each other was an understatement. Over a thirty-year period that they were best friends, and Nancy told me that she would do anything for Lucy. If Lucy asked, Nancy was always there to lend a hand and more.

When Nancy was dying, Lucy's pain was evident and deep. It was Lucy who was at Nancy's side when I had to go to California for two weeks on business in January, just after Nancy's diagnosis. Only a few days later, it was Lucy who was at Nancy's side when Nan went into "A" fib and had to be rushed to the University of Chicago Hospital. It was Lucy who consoled my brother-in-law, David, when we all did not think Nancy would live through that weekend, though she did.

It was Lucy who would show up at Nancy's front door with a hot casserole for the family's dinner or Nancy's favorite sliced beef and Provolone cheese on a buttery croissant from the Indiana Deli. It was Lucy who popped in for a visit just to listen to Nancy's fears. Lucy went out of her way to run errands, bring Nancy flowers, and just sit with her while she slept. Perhaps it was Lucy's desire to WILL Nancy well in addition to all the prayers that were being said for Nan.

We all wanted to give Nancy hope, even when our hopes were ash.

For anyone who has been handed the ticket by fate to ride on the rollercoaster of a loved one's dying days, my heart and soul cries for you. It is the most difficult burden in the world to watch the person you love the most on earth, crawl painfully toward death. We tell ourselves that death is inevitable. We know that this is our end goal. Intellectually, we understand death. We think. The emotional experience is another matter. We are angry and sad. Sorrow-filled and compassionate. We are irrational and at moments have great flashes of brilliance and understanding God's purpose for us during our loved one's dance with death.

Is this the time to test our souls? Are we reaping the old seeds we have sown? Are we being given a chance to do what is right by our loved ones? Is this a time of forgiveness? A time to forgive them? For them to forgive us? A time of confession? Or is it time to pour our love onto them in an unceasing flow?

I believe it is all of these. These times are precious opportunities to not only do the right thing, but to expand our own humanness and express our spirituality. It is a time to pray and a time to listen. Sometimes we are gifted with the recovery of our child, parent, or sister. Sometimes, God calls them home. As painful as it is for us to live without our loved one, we must, as my mother said, "Understand that God allowed Nancy (your loved one) to stay on earth as long as HE could stand it."

During those days and weeks as winter moved into spring, Lucy revealed to us all how deeply she loved Nancy and to what lengths she would go to make Nancy's final months just a bit less painful.

For five months, we all wanted to believe that the doctors were wrong. We would not accept that Nancy was dying and that there was no cure to a cancer that had no known origin (Adeno-carcinoma), nor that it was metastasizing.

When something this staggeringly impossible to believe happens to your loved one, the shock alone impairs our ability to accept the truth of the situation. No matter how many times we go to the Web and investigate the symptoms and the prognoses or talk to doctor after specialist, after doctor, denial is the only armor for our pain.

As my husband had often said, "Nancy was the closest thing there is to a perfect human being." If there was a nearly spotless soul, a font of unconditional love and a spirit of endless giving and caring, that was Nancy. For all of us to lose such a light in the world was a tragedy.

For Lucy, it was losing a part of her being.

Therefore, it was only natural that one of the first people that Nancy would appear to after her death, would be Lucy.

It was on a Wednesday, on my day off from my brother-in-law's dental office that I was sitting at my computer working on a new novel when my email "pinged" to let me know that I had just received a new email. Once I finished the paragraph I was writing, I checked my email.

The subject matter said: "Call me...NOW!"

I instantly read Lucy's email to me and what I read made my neck hairs stand on end. In the body of the email, she said that Nancy had just appeared to her while she was working on her computer. She asked me to call.

I immediately telephoned Lucy and believe me; her voice was quaking. "I'm still in shock," Lucy said. "I am not the kind of person that has these experiences and I have always been not quite so sure that these things were real. It is easy to de-bunk the debunkable. But this was clearly not my imagination! I was wide awake! Nancy stood right in front of me while I was working on my computer. This just happened only a few minutes ago, Cath! I cannot believe it."

"What did she look like?" I asked. "Was she transparent? Ghostlike? Did you see her out of the corner of your eye?"

"No. She was as real as you or I. It was like she was alive. She was wearing her regular clothes like I had seen her wearing a hundred times. But that is not the scary part."

"That's not?" This alone was frightening enough for me. I could not imagine that the encounter got worse.

"She reached out and stuck her hand down into my chest and put her fingers around my heart and said, "'I'll be seeing you soon.'"

In all the submissions of angel stories and visitations from departed family and friends, not once had I ever heard of the dead person's spirit being able to put their own hand inside a living person's body. Maybe it has happened, but it has got to be pretty darn rare. I was stunned. She told me she was shaking so hard she thought she might drop the phone.

To calm Lucy, I asked her more questions. "Did she say anything else?"

"Nothing. Right after she said what I told you, she vanished. Just like that. Then I emailed you. I did not know where you were."

I then asked Lucy if there were any problems with her heart. She told me there were not.

"Lucy, I do not ever take these things lightly. I believe Nancy came to you to give you this warning about your health. Promise me you will make an appointment to see a doctor very soon and have some blood tests and an EKG. Something is wrong with your heart. Nancy loved you dearly. She also knew you as well as you know yourself. She probably knew she would have to scare the dickens out of you to get you to go have your heart checked." "It worked. I am scared. Why would she be telling me that she would be seeing me soon? I am in good health. There is nothing wrong. Do you think they know the future when they get to heaven?"

"I do not know. But this is a very strong warning. I also think it is heart related because she put her hand into your chest and held her heart. This was not a love pat on the shoulder. This is serious."

"I agree."

"Good. See the doctor."

A few weeks later, Lucy had her heart checked and other than a few changes in her diet and an increase in exercise that was recommended, everything appeared quite normal.

Both Lucy and I tried to pretend that Nancy's "visit" was not a dire warning. We both believe that the measurement of "time" in heaven or The Other Side is not what it is on earth. Therefore, "soon" might be twenty more years on earth. That is a good rationalization, isn't it? We also tried to reason that Nancy putting her hand on Lucy's heart was a sign that she loved Lucy very much. It was a "sisterly" sign; you are close in my heart always. That kind of thing.

One year later, nearly to the week of Nancy's visitation, Lucy was gravely ill and had to be hospitalized. She had trouble with her pancreas. And her heart. She was in the hospital for three days. When she returned home, she had a renewed sense of purpose about her health. She drastically altered her diet and lost a significant amount of weight. She started riding her bike again. She got more rest and took breaks when she needed them.

On her last checkup, Lucy's doctor was more than pleased with the improvements he found in Lucy's heart and her overall health.

I believe that Nancy's "visit" to Lucy was indeed a warning about her health. Only God knows if Lucy would continue down a path to ill-health if she had not changed some things in her daily routines to make these improvements. I do not necessarily believe that Nancy was warning Lucy that death was imminent, but I do believe that Nancy used "shock value" to get her point across. Nan did that kind of thing in life to get my attention when I needed strong guidance. It only makes sense to me that she would do the same on The Other Side.

I have read that we take our personalities with us when we move on to the next life. We talk the same and act the same. We are still ourselves. I think that is why it is important for all of us to take stock of ourselves from time to time and ask, "Am I being all that I can be? Am I helping others when it is possible to do so? Am I being as loving as I should? Am I being strong enough to do what is right for me?"

The last question is a tough one because it may cause us to make significant changes in our lives and lifestyle to force ourselves to evolve to our highest human potential.

Even though Lucy did not believe such spirit visitations happened before Nancy's visit, she was strong enough and wise enough not to discount the warning. She followed through. She changed her life which will prolong her life. For me, her friend, I am grateful she listened to Nancy when she came to call.

Six

DREAM WARNINGS OR IMAGINATION?

Dreams are the super-highway for angels and departed loved ones to "get through" the quagmire of human thoughts and anxieties to talk to us. In our dreaming state, our everyday, overloaded brains are supposedly resting. The opposite is true.

Psychiatrists and dream therapists tell us that we "download" our daily mental tasks and experience deeper-emotional and psychological issues during deeper sleep, or REM sleep. If you have never kept a journal of your nightly dreams, it is a fascinating process to look inside your emotional self and ferret out fears, concerns, anxieties, and personality issues. Your dreams are about you.

The dream world has fascinated scientists and theologians for years. Most of us know about Freud and Carl Jung's research on dreams. Freud believed that our dream state revealed repressed wishes. Carl Jung believed the anima, the shadow, and the animus, were symbolic figures in our dreams of repressed attitudes. He believed that dreams were highly personal. G. William Dumhoff, the noted dream researcher and who studied at the University of Miami with Calvin Hall, he believes that dreams represent our waking concerns.

'Meaning' has to do with coherence and with systematic relations to other variables, and in that regard, dreams do have meaning. Furthermore, they are very "revealing" of what is on our minds. We have shown that 75 to 100 dreams from a person give us a very good psychological portrait of that individual. Give us 1000 dreams over a couple of decades and we can give you a profile of the person's mind that is almost as individualized and accurate as her or his fingerprints."

This is what the scientific community gives us as an explanation of our dreams. My guess is that if I were to go to one of these researchers and report a dream visitation from one of my very dead relatives, they would explain it to me as a symbol of my un-requited grief over the loss of my loved one.

I'll buy that.

Except for the fact that in my case and in the case of those people who write to me or speak with me about their experiences being visited by an actual angel or a dead relative, they were being given a specific message upon which they acted.

When a departed loved one visits us to tell us that they are happy in their new home in heaven and they just want us to know that we are loved, there is peace in our lives. We finally have the comfort we need to continue with our lives without them.

To the scientists I will say, "Okay, it's a stretch for me, but I will concede that on this one, you could be right."

Except…I say.

There are the times when an angel or a loved one comes to us in a dream and gives us a warning. A few days or even months later, this warning is proved out.

Perhaps our angel tells us that we need to see the doctor. We do not go. We have a heart attack. We were warned and we did not do anything about it. We listened to the scientists and rationalized that our dream was "just a dream." It did not mean anything.

Then there are those of us who do believe that something more powerful is going on in our dream state than just "download processing of our brain chips."

We DO listen to our angel and we go to the doctor.

This is precisely what happened to me.

My sister, Nancy, visited me in a dream about six months after her death. I was grieving terribly over her death. I was sad and anxious. In the dream she stood next to me by my bedside and said, *"Go to the doctor for your heart is broken."*

The next morning, I remembered the dream as so real it was as if I could have touched her. She looked much younger than she had when she died. She was beautiful and stood strong, tall, and healthy. Her voice was very emphatic and it was the tone she used when she would not take "no" for an answer. I never liked that tone when she used it.

The next day, I called the cardiologist's office and made an appointment. I was a new patient because I had never been to the cardiologist. There was nothing wrong with my heart. Not a thing.

The receptionist bought my explanation that I simply felt it was time for me to get a checkup.

I went for the regular stress test and did the treadmill thing, which since I walk on a treadmill every day and have worked out doing something of one kind or another since I was thirteen, I did well on the treadmill. The physician's assistant said that most thirty-year-olds did not do as well.

However--

Sure enough, when they stuck that ultra sound doomajiggy thing on my chest, there it was. Arrhythmia.

I was stunned.

The doctor came in and he was surprised as well. The first thing he asked was about my stress level. On a scale of one to ten, I was at about a seventeen. Since I knew the doctor as a friend, he truly understood everything I was going through since Nancy's death. He nodded. Then he asked what symptoms I had.

"None."

He lowered my chart. "Then why are you here? Why now?"

Yep. I had to explain that Nancy came to me in a dream and told me to get a check-up. I also told him that this was the third time in my life that either an angel or a dead relative had come to me about my health. Twice before, my life was literally saved and I had emergency surgery.

"This is not so drastic," the doctor said. I was instructed to reduce my stress immediately. Keep up the exercise, sleep more (yeah, sure), and eat balanced meals.

So, what else was new?

I was given some pills to help if my heart went into arrhythmia again.

For those of us whose life has been saved by a dream warning or if we have saved someone else's emotional well-being or their physical well-being because we were visited in a dream by an angel, we will probably always be skeptical of the scientific community who try to tell us that what we experienced was not real.

What we KNOW is that we get REAL results.

Our lives have been changed because we believed what we saw. Our visitations were real to us. These messages and warnings altered our divine path. We can go on to help others who need us. We may save another person, all because we listened to a divine intervention.

Seven

ANGELIC WARNINGS PRE-COVID-19

I n 2019, *the Universe altered. The war between good and evil over, around and through the planet Earth amped up and so did angelic interventions.* I conducted research with energy healers, psychics, angelic channelers, astrologers and prognosticators. In early 2019, they stated that the energies and frequencies revealed that something dire was about to come into the earth's reality, but no one knew what it was. No fingers were pointing to a war and certainly not to a pandemic.

In August of 2019, I experienced one of the most profound angelic visitations of my life. My very first angel visitation was when I was three years old. Now, I was over seventy. I have had a lot of visitations, messages and interactions with the celestial realm, Jesus, Mother Mary, nearly every Archangel, but the story you are about to read still gives me chills of wonder and awe.

There is no doubt for me that humanity is protected and loved by God/Source/ All That There Is.

THE TEN THOUSAND

This story took place mid-summer 2019, and on this week, there was no imminent danger or situation going on in my personal life. I had, however, been feeling the need to pray for the world. It was almost as if I heard the earth crying for help. We had experienced a very long, cold, dreary, grey, depressing winter. Spring came slowly. June was cold and rainy and reminded me more of March than any other time of year. It certainly was not the lovely satin Junes I ever remembered.

Every Friday night just about sundown or before, I light tea light candles in a beautiful collection of crystal rose bowls I have collected since 1986. With each candle I say a prayer for all my deceased family, friends, and the world. I give gratitude for the life I have and the abundance of God's graces that have been bestowed on me. Back in 1986, I only had grandparents and friends who died in Vietnam. Today, this candle lighting and remembering every dead person's name whom I want to remember is a real mind-memory trick, I will tell you.

On this night, I had felt a significant weight of sadness about the world. This was energy that clung to me all evening long. None of this sense of despair was from television news or reading newspaper or magazines, because I turned off all media outlets after so many recent family members' deaths at the advice of my grief counselor.

This night as I went to bed and said my prayers, I asked Jesus if there was any way that he could give me a sign, send a message, give me a "download dump," I would sure appreciate it. If there was something, he wanted me to do for the world, I needed desperately to know what that was and how to do it.

As a rule, I do not sleep all that well any more. I used to hit the bed and not know a thing till morning. I cannot say that this insomnia is due to not having a whole lot to do. After working ten hours a day in the dental office and writing three books and a couple screenplays every year, pretty much---I'm tired. I need my sleep. Unfortunately, I awake in the middle of the night and read for two, three or four hours. This is great for my mind and my constant accumulation of knowledge and shores up my list of book titles on the bookshelves. I chalked it up to age. Then I did the wise thing and asked my angels why I could not sleep.

Their answer was loud and clear. "We're trying to talk to you."

Yeah? Well, I am trying to sleep.

So, it was on this night that I woke at 2:22. I pay particular attention to the moments when I hear a voice in my head say, "Look at the clock." When the numbers are repetitive, 3:33; 4:44; 5:55, etc. I know the angels are trying to contact me.

I fell back asleep after 4:44 because I had looked at the clock and double-checked that it was 4:44. At the time I did register that it was odd to have woken at 2:22 and then got sleepy at 4:44.

I should have paid better attention.

I heard a knock. Not a knock at the front door but on my bedroom door. Then I heard a man's voice. "Catherine."

This was the mellow tones of a caring, almost honeyed-sweet male voice. Not harsh or gruff; not deep and not that velvety "radio" voice a lot of male actors, television anchors and announcers have. There was only one person I knew who possessed a voice that harmonious and yet strong. Jesus.

He was standing at the doorway to my bedroom looking down at me. He wore a shimmering white tunic that always looks like a blend of linen and silk with a beige fabric tie around his waist. The sleeves were long and covered his arms, but his hands are always visible.

That is another thing. Whenever Jesus appears to me, I check him out. My eyes go right to his hands where I expect to see the nail scars. If those hands are not his, then I know I have got to get rid of the imposter.

It was Jesus.

"Come. Follow me," he said.

Jesus commands. I act.

I got up and followed him out of my bedroom which is opposite the dining room. (Told you it was an old house.) We went to the foyer which is the size of a coat closet.

He said, "Open the door."

I opened the door. My opening the door was a sign of my surrender to his wishes; his leadership. I did not question. I trusted he was guiding me for my highest good. Once you determine that your angels, ascended masters, and Beings of Light are from the Light, your trust is a key ingredient in the extent of the information you will receive in your vision, download or visitation.

"There's someone to see you," he said.

"And you're not enough?" I asked. Yeah. I know. I am always cracking a joke. Even with my angels, Jesus and spirit guides. Hey, they do it to me. I have been told a great many times, that I take life too seriously. I must lighten up, they say. It is true. They say that to me.

For twenty-five years I thought I was one of a kind in that department—being too serious about my mission and my spiritual self. Just two nights before this experience and visitation from Jesus, I was reading my fifth or sixth Delores Cannon book. Delores Cannon is the creator of QHHT--Quantum Healing Hypnosis Technique. In her hypnosis sessions she talks to the client's Higher Self/subconscious/Oversoul or the Christ Conscious. I had just read a section in which she was taking a client back to a former lifetime. This person had all kinds of physical and emotional issues. The line that jumped out at me said: "Miss Z takes life too seriously. She needs to lighten up."

Those were the EXACT words I had been told when I went to the Council of Nine one night when my sister Nancy was alive and she was pleading for my life. (This story is found in my second angel book, *Divine Nudges*).

"Look!" Jesus demanded and pointed to my front lawn.

I have a large front lawn and in front of it is a narrow street. No curbs, gutters, or sidewalks. It was only recently paved for the first time ever. This land I live on had once been an apple orchard. Across from my front lawn is a monster sized golf course which was built over one hundred years ago. The pine trees scrape clouds. It is majestic, ethereal and one of the most beautiful parks I have ever seen.

Back in 1949 when this little area, not a subdivision, since it is just one street, the lots were being sold. Each was 7/8 of an acre.

My parents had met in Pinehurst, North Carolina near Fort Bragg, where my father was an Army captain and my mother a hospital dietician. Before my father left for the Pacific theater, they played golf in Pinehurst every chance they got.

Building a house overlooking a golf course was their dream.

My mother, with a keen eye for beauty and aesthetics, looked at every lot on this street. She stood on the vacant grounds and determined where her kitchen window would be. She chose this lot because of the view.

From this kitchen window, the view is nearly a mile in the distance. It travels over the 5th Tee, a green, down a par 5 fairway and up a very high hill.

"When I die, heaven will not be as beautiful as these Elysian Fields," she always said.

When my father went to the County Recorder to purchase the lot, he was told it had been sold the Sunday prior. My mother was heartsick. No other lot on the street would do. She told my father they would look for a lake lot instead. Having the water for her view would be second best.

One month later my father was in his law office when a man came to see him. It was the man who had bought the golf course lot my mother wanted. He asked my father if he was still interested in the lot. My father assured him he was, but why did the man want to sell?

"My wife has been diagnosed with cancer. I need the money for her treatments."

My father empathized with the man and together they went to the County Recorder's office to finalize the sale of the lot to my father.

That is how this land came to be the Lanigan home.

I had to tell you that whole story for you to understand the magnitude and magnificence of the sight I was to see.

In the depths of my psyche, I have probably always known this land was magical, but in more recent years I have come to discover that there are several portals on this property and especially on the golf course directly out the window my mother referred as Elysian Fields. I now wonder, what did she see when she gazed out that window? More than trees and lovely fairway? Did she see angels?

In my front yard are two, 72-year-old Maple trees and two Adirondack chairs and a table where my deceased husband, Jed and I used to sit and watch the golfers play on pretty weekend afternoons.

I was shocked at the sight in my front yard.

Sitting in one chair was Jed. He did not appear transparent or ghostlike, but he was younger and very healthy. I was struck by how casually he was conversing with the angels as if they all hung around together like buddies.

Standing in front of him were three enormous angels. At first, I thought the three were Archangels, but they were not. These angels were dressed in white gowns and their wings were huge and all white. They literally gleamed and glistened not in the sun, but from their own radiance.

"Here is the answer to your prayers, Catherine. God has heard you. So have they all," Jesus said.

He touched my shoulder and urged me to walk outside.

I stood on the steps, Jesus behind me. Jed turned around and waved. He blew me a kiss. Then he pointed to the golf course.

From the Fifth Tee, filling the green, down that long, and wide fairway which is bordered by fifty-year-old Willow trees, pine, oaks, Black Walnut and maple trees, and a reflective lake, were ten thousand angels. They were wing to wing, all dressed in white diaphanous gowns, their feet hovering just above the grass. I could not hear their song, but I felt it in my heart.

They were singing, "We are here." They said it over and over and with no additions to the lyrics. The harmony and music were astounding and it chimed its symphony all through my body to my cells. It was uplifting, life-changing and unforgettable.

They were here to love, to help, to protect the earth and to carry each one of our prayers for the healing of the earth and all the hollow hearts of lost humans to God. They were here to bring a message of hope.

Hope for a better world. Hope for the day when all of us raise our vibrations, our frequency and open our hearts; whatever set of semantics you want to use that you feel comfortable with.

This is their message: Love conquers all hatred. All violence. All ignorance. All power-mongering. Love was Jesus' message to earthlings. Love is the base of every religion, spiritual consciousness on earth.

Love is the glue that holds the universe together. It is more than divine consciousness. It is the Divine Heart.

The era of the world being governed by a myriad of misguided mind-sets is over. The world is being made new.

Live, believe, think with your heart first and only.

Little did I know THEN the prediction I was being given. I thought my vision was of a solitary nature, meant only for me. It was not. It was for the world. As I write this now in the center of Covid-19 lockdown, I know what this virus is about. This is God speaking to us.

If we do not stop polluting the earth with our hatred, crude, hurtful and violent words, and greedy actions, we will lose this planet. We have lost it before due to our negative thoughts and emotions. The Great Flood destroyed Atlantis, Lemuria, and more islands and land masses than we know about, but are yet to be discovered.

I saw his first battalion. And he has got a whole lot more angels.

In Matthew 26:53-54 Jesus said, "Put your sword back where it belongs. All who use swords are destroyed by swords. Don't you realize that I am able right now to call upon my Father, and twelve companies—more, if I want them---of fighting angels would be here battle-ready? But if I did that, how would the Scriptures come true that say this is the way it has to be?"

The ten thousand angels, that night were telling me they were that they were prepared to fight. *"We are here."*

I also realize upon more analysis of the visitation that the angels' feet never touched the ground. They hovered just above the ground. They were not walking on the earth but were in proximity.

Humans are the "boots on the ground" in this battle for planet earth. The angels will help us if we ASK them for help. They are at the ready, armed with enough love to shift our consciousness; shift the trajectory of our timeline to one of peace, love, happiness, and joy. Those of us who CHOOSE wisely, I would think, will make the shift.

Not everyone will make shift. And that is okay. Perhaps they have more attachment to this dimension. They may have lessons to learn or experiences they want to immerse their consciousness in. That is why we have free choice. They will get there in their own time.

Over two-thousand years ago, Jesus said love was the answer. It still is.

Eight

DOVETAILING TIMELINES

Author Note: Quantum physics tells us that there is no linear time, except in our 3D dimension. Physics tells us that time is ever-present. The Past is the present and the present is the future and this is why scientists can experiment with moving objects, even people back to the past or forward to the future. There are books and videos, pod cast interviews by people who claim they are from the future---or at least one future time line. There are many parallel worlds that can be our future. But my story here is one about the past and how it came to me through my angels and affected my life in the present.

I wrote the story just as it is presented here.

MIRACULOUS MEDAL OF MARY

July 19, 2020

Author Note: It is important to this story that you take note of the date here today. More about that as this story unfolds.

Yesterday, I was rifling through a drawer in my deceased husband's old dresser; a place I had not been for years. I found an old, rusty looking Miraculous Medal of Mary. I cleaned it up and noticed it was not silver, but probably just nickel.

Finding it was interesting timing to me, because my deceased sister, Nancy's, mother-in-law had passed away only a week prior. In the process of going through her house we found a lovely Miraculous Medal of Mary on a chain.

In both instances, these medals were the property of non-Catholics.

However, for now, I am going to take you back to the past.

The history of the Miraculous Medal dates back to the night of July 18, 1830 in Paris, France at the Daughters of Charity Convent where a young, twenty-four-year-old nun, Sister Catherine Laboure slept. Suddenly, a mysterious child appeared in her room and wakened Sister Catherine. The child urged her to get up and follow her to the convent's chapel.

Sister Catherine walked into the empty chapel and saw the beautiful, young, and radiant Blessed Virgin/Mother Mary sitting in a chair. I can only imagine how stunned and humbled Catherine had to be at that point. Overwhelmed a bit? Thinking she had lost her mind? Was this a dream or had she walked into the past? Or even the future?

She walked over to Mother Mary, who did not stir. She knelt beside Mary and put her hands in Mary's lap.

I do not know about you, but I would have been in tears and breathless at this point. But not Catherine. According to what Catherine reported about that night, she spoke with Mary for several hours. What we would not all give for a recording of THAT conversation!

However, the end of it was that Mary promised to return to visit Catherine and at that point, she would give Catherine instructions about her life's "mission."

Interestingly to me, was the fact that the "child" stayed with the two women all night. The "child" led Catherine back to her room. At that moment, Catherine heard the clock strike 2:00 am. July, 19.

Yesterday, July 18, 2020 while I cleaned up this very old Miraculous Mary Medal, I pondered the interesting symbols that are on the back of the medal. I had not seen a medal like this one since the early 1950's when I was a child. Also, my husband was not Catholic. But he had kept this medal, which must have belonged to one of his Catholic aunts for over sixty years.

I finished out my day of writing and went to sleep on the night of the 18th.

I woke up in the middle of the night last night, at 2:00 AM July 19, 2020. I needed a drink of water. It was nearly 100 degrees the day before and a thunderstorm was rolling in. As I stood at the kitchen window looking out at the lightning in the distance, I remembered the Miraculous Medal. I was suddenly struck with the angelic message to go the computer and look up the history of the Medal. This was an odd thought for me because it was not often, I worked at the computer at night. But the urging to investigate was strong. This was the same kind of guidance I often received from my angels and guides. This was significant. However, little did I know I was being guided at precisely the time of night and the day of the year that Sister Catherine Laboure met with Mother Mary.

I was agog when I read the information on the internet. This timing was not coincidence. My angels were talking to me and urging me. Just as importantly, I took the "action" to sit down and chronicle these events. They were insistent that I tell you this story of the amazing Miraculous Medal of Mary.

Let us go back to Paris, 1830.

On the night of November 27,1830, Catherine had another visitation from Mother Mary. The vision was Mary, "In all her perfect beauty," as radiant as a sunrise, standing in a position just as we see in the Medal today. There were rays of colored lights shooting out from the palms of her hands. Blessed Virgin told Sister Catherine, ***The rays symbolize the graces I shed upon those who ask for them.***

In the vision, Mary stood atop the entire world, crushing a serpent under her feet. As Catherine stared at the dazzling Mary, the vision altered to include the words that are inscribed on the Medal. "O Mary, conceived without sin, pray for us who have recourse to thee."

The word "recourse" is not used in contemporary nomenclature. I had always defined it as a plea or prayer, which it is. But in J.I. Rodale's *The Synonym Finder,* the first descriptor is "access." This is an entirely different viewpoint than simply a plea. "Access" implies that one has a personal relationship with Mary. It implies faith on the petitioner's part. Though Mother Mary appeared to Catherine over a hundred and ninety years ago, this message is just as meaningful today, or more so, than it was then.

We, who need help, must believe we are worthy to receive these gifts. These rays of blessings that Mary will bestow on us are not "luck." They are not whimsical. They are real---if we believe.

My mother always said, "I receive a lot of miracles in my life because I expect them." My mother did not just pray for them, she lived her life as if the miracle had already happened. She planned on miracles. She planned on God's graces and she got them.

The last message that Sister Catherine received was Mary saying to her: "Have a medal struck upon this model. Those who wear it will receive great graces, especially if they wear it around their neck."

To be clear, if you go look up this Medal, the flip side of the Medal is lovely as well, but that was not part of Sister Catherine's vision. However, here is what it means.

There is a huge M in the center with a cross coming out the top forming a stabilizing bar under the M. The M is for Mary and the Cross symbolizes Jesus. Around the entire symbol are 12 stars, representing the 12 apostles, who formed the first church.

At the very bottom are two hearts. The heart on the right, pierced by a sword, is the Immaculate Heart of Mary. The heart on the left is the Sacred Heart of Jesus.

The flames at the bottom represent the burning love that Jesus and Mary have for us.

The back of the Medal was designed by the Marian Fathers of the Immaculate Conception. It was struck in 1832 and today has worldwide devotion.

Shortly after Sister Catherine and her priest got Catherine's vision struck into a medal, she was able to distribute the medal to all the people of her area.

Within months the **Bubonic Plague** hit all of Europe. It was as devastating to the people then as the Covid-19 is to us now. Perhaps more so. BUT---- all those who had received and worn a Miraculous Medal of Mary did not get the plague. They did not die. They were protected.

Mary's Medal won its name, MIRACULOUS MEDAL OF MARY because it saved many lives during that plague.

There was no coincidence that I was compelled to react to my angels' guidance, nor to feeling driven to write this story of finding this long-lost medal.

The lockdowns of 2020 have passed and though there is speculation that another plandemic or pandemic is about to descend, I believe there are enough of us who will stand together and prayerfully bring in those graces that Mother Mary promised and annihilate suffering and death. We have the power within us and the celestial realms are here to aid us.

Nine

IT'S ALL ABOUT FREQUENCY

I *cannot even count the number of times I have been* asked how do I connect with my angels? What is the trick? Is it a special prayer? A vegan diet? I have seen scammers on the internet, on podcasts and in print who guarantee they can teach a person to contact an angel and get results.

As once was said so aptly, "There are no guarantees in life."

What has been demonstrated in almost every story here in this book are instances of communication through frequency. You did not see it? It is there. In the wishes, the petitions, the prayers, and the deep inner knowingness of each of these experiencers, I will call them, that someone, some-thing would come to their aide.

I recently had a conversation with a woman who wanted my advice. She felt she was not advancing on her spiritual path to the degree that she should. She was a Reiki Master and had indeed helped many people to heal. Truly, I felt she had a gift for healing. She meditated daily. She had taken courses in just about every spiritual practice I could name.

Yet, she was frustrated and disappointed, she said. She was admittedly not happy with herself.

I continued asking her questions, because as far as I could tell, she was quite knowledgeable, advanced in her skills and had many pleased clients. She said she had prayed, pleaded with the Universe, and begged. But she was not getting the answer she wanted.

Once I determined that she was not after the usual requests of: "I want to win the lottery" or "find my soul-mate" desires, I stopped, I had one final question.

"Are you wanting to SEE an angel in person?" I asked.

"Yes," she said anxiously.

I asked, "Why?"

"I want proof God hears me."

I realized that this woman was coming from a place of desperation. There was no inner "knowingness," no faith that Source would send her whatever she needed. As spiritual as she claimed to be, she was nothing of the sort.

She was a skilled practitioner in the healing arts. So are medical doctors, nurses, dentists, etc.

She had missed the one vital aspect of spirituality. Faith.

Back in the late 1950's was a popular song called *I Believe*. A few of the lyrics were: *I believe for every drop of rain that falls; a flower grows. I believe that in the dark somewhere, a candle glows. I believe that for everyone that goes astray, someone will come to show the way.*

Basically, that was the song. It has stayed with me all my life.

Angels show their presence to us in so many ways. One obvious one is repeating numbers. Watch your clock diligently and every time you see 111 or 222, 333, etc. say "Thank you to your angels for watching over you." I have found the more I talk to my angels and act as if they are in the room participating with me in my activities, the more they are around.

If you walk into a closed room and feel a brush or drift of air past you, could be an angel wing. I am not saying it always is, but thank your angel. See if it happens again.

That shadow in the corner of your eye, or the golden sunlight that lingers or seems to glow brighter and then fade as it falls through the window, that can be an angel's energy.

Angels do not always show up in white robes, gold belts and ten-foot-wide wings, but they can and do. Most of their visits are when you are sleeping. This is when the frequencies of your mind and their frequency are most likely to link and meld. Because so many of us do not journal our dreams upon waking, we either forget what happened or claim we did not dream at all. Thus, we believe there are no angels; nothing celestial is happening in our lives; and we continue down a path of disappointment that is surely depressing and non-productive spiritually.

The celestial realms are active in our timeline in history right now. Humanity has the chance to integrate with this space outside of our dimension and the angels want to give us a leg up. There is a lot of information being given to humans through our thoughts, dreams, visions, and meditations.

Some information that is coming through reveals that there had been a great deal of trickery in which humans have been the dupes. We have allowed this to happen every time we give up our freedoms. Freedom of speech is one. There are many when you contemplate the extent of the control being exercised in our society today.

This is not the way of the Divine.

When you delve deep enough, go back to the beginning of Creation, God gave humans Free Will. Free Choice. Freedom.

Our Creator envisioned freedom for humans. WE created this enslavement we suffer by our choices. Bit by bit, we were either disillusioned, duped or tricked into believing that we were taking the high road. We were programmed to accept being comfortable at the expense of loss of yet another freedom.

I believe this place, this space where this 3D earth has devolved into, can be changed. It is up to us. Love will win.

Love conquers all. How many times have we heard that? Apparently, not enough. The strongest force/energy in the Universe is love.

If we send love to every man, woman, child, government, country, and especially to the warring nations, we negate hatred.

The manifestation force of prayer is real. Prayer with the intention of love, can cure disease. It has saved many from battles, war, death. Love is in our hearts. Our hearts can alter the timeline path that humanity has created. This programmed reality of 3D where we sit on the verge of World

War III and possible nuclear annihilation, has never been leveled on humanity before. Do we have to go this far to fall to our knees to finally SEE the divine in our lives?

We need to pay attention to the little things in our lives that prove the divine is here and working on our behalf.

There are many now who are coming forward to help us all see the truth. They are seeing, talking to, and taking notes on what the angels are telling them about the world now.

I am not the only one who wants to share my stories with you.

MY SPECIAL ANGEL

Author's Note: This story was sent to me by Pat Wolla. Thank you so much, Pat. Pat's story is one about frequencies meeting head on. Hers was a long journey, but when she finally met her angel, she had truly explored the unknown.

After reading Mary Summer Rain's book, *Spirit Song*, I started making regular trips every fall to visit Colorado with the first trip in 1993. And, also, at this time, I became involved in metaphysics. I joined a group called *Genesis* in Fort Worth, Texas and met my new friend, Rod. Rod had been studying metaphysics for over thirty years and was very knowledgeable. Rod and I would get together every Saturday afternoon and spend many hours talking about spirituality. After a few sessions working with him, learning to meditate, I finally succeeded in having my first out-of-body experiences. This was a new and exciting adventure for me.

In 1994, I went on a trip to Colorado and was having a wonderful time but, finally it was time to go home. I was standing at the gas station filling my SUV with gas looking at Pikes Peak and observing a beautiful aura on the mountaintop. Suddenly, the thought came to me that I needed to see to my friend, Roxanne, who was my masseuse and whom I had met a couple of years before. I called Roxanne and arranged for a meeting.

When I arrived at Roxanne's house, I had the opportunity to meet Mary Summer Rain's husband, Bill, who was also Roxanne's client. Meeting Bill was very exciting because I believed it was a way to move forward toward my dream of meeting Mary herself. However, I did not impose upon Bill to introduce me to Mary because I felt it would be rude to push.

I found Bill to be a very charming person and I enjoyed our visit. However, our meeting was cut short because Bill had another engagement.

Then in 1995, one evening I received a call from my new friend, Carole Bourdo, who created the art work and layout for Mary Rain's book covers. She informed me that Bill had committed suicide. I was shocked and devastated.

Carol then explained the details of the tragedy to me. The tragedy was so horrendous and sad that I was in tears for the rest of the evening. I could not sleep that night. I had nightmares and fitful dreams. At one point, I dreamed that I was in our living room and my brother was present. We were simply chatting about ordinary things, when suddenly I told him that I could not stay.

It was then that I traveled out of my body and was flying through the universe.

I know this sounds strange but it happened to me. My consciousness/spirit left my physical body. I could see my body as I rose higher and higher. I felt light and free and full of endless possibilities.

I met a woman who appeared to be in her middle forties, dressed in a gray business suit. I told her that I had come to The Other Side to meet my friend, Bill, who had just passed over. I told the woman that I needed desperately to speak with him.

She said to me, "I have someone back on earth to meet and have been looking for him."

The woman said nothing else and there were no significant messages that she told me. Today, I find it an interesting and exceptional encounter. This woman was apparently still living her life on earth, just as I was. We were fellow astral-travelers.

After meeting the woman in the suit, I continued my search for Bill but was not able to find him. I remember that I saw other things on my search but, unfortunately, do not remember all of them.

Suddenly, I saw a man who was absolutely the most beautiful person I had ever seen. He was tall, dressed in white clothes with a gold belt at the waist and wearing brown sandals. His hair was shoulder-length, brown and with a gold head band. He radiated immense love and rays of golden light shimmered from his being. I was stunned with his beauty, to the point that I could barely speak. I remembered that Rod had always told me to ask questions when I met a being during an out-of-body experience. Truthfully, most of those prior times, I almost always forgot to ask anything. But, not this time.

This time I managed to stutter, "Who are you?"

He answered, "I'm known as Gabriel."

He had no more than told me his name when instantly, I returned to my body with such a swiftness, I felt I was being sucked from one universe to another.

When I awoke and realized I was back in my body, I did not know if I should be happy or sad.

Every aspect of that encounter has been burned into my memory. It is impossible for me to ever forget any of it. I know it was real and true. There was nothing about it that was a dream or my imagination.

I had met one of the four mighty Archangels. I believe absolutely that he is watching over me and protecting me. He is my Special Angel and his name is Gabriel.

Ten

ARE YOU PAYING ATTENTION YET?

Pre-Pandemic

May, 2019 Spring.

Every year I carry on my mother's tradition of throwing a Kentucky Derby party. I still make her very old Southern recipe for Mint Juleps which I have pitted against some real know-it-alls who think they have the best recipe, but sorry. Mother's Mobile, Alabama recipe which she got from her mother and was circa WWI, still reigns. And nope, I am not sharing. But I will tell you, it is time consuming and most people today would not expend the effort. However, now that I have been doing this for over a decade back here again in Indiana, my guests are spoiled rotten.

I have a fun "pool" for betting. The week before the race, I scour the Derby web site. I size up the horses and listen to the pod casts and interviews of the jockeys. I fill the house with red roses I get at the grocery store…or stores and make an array of Southern appetizers that both my mom and dad loved. Let's just say there's a lot of Southern hickory smoked and sugar-coated bacon and leave it at that.

The ladies wear hats, and the men bring the betting bucks. It is a very fun night.

I believe it is important for us to live each moment we can with fun and create happiness for others. Because there are no guarantees in life; and everything changes from hour to hour, why not live our lives? There is more to this existence than just going to work, paying the bills, and waiting to die.

The truth is we never die. We are energy beings and our lives go on forever even as we return to God, the One Source, the Creator. Throughout the universes, planets, dimensions, and parallel existences, we are continually learning and experiencing.

On earth, though we learn skills, utilize talents God has given us, our underlying or overlying lesson is to love and forgive. Without forgiveness both to those who have hurt us, defiled us, tortured us; if we do not also forgive ourselves, we have not reached the goal of unconditional love.

Love thy neighbor as thyself. We must love ourselves first. And how many of us do that?

I am just as much as fault as the next person for not loving myself enough. Taking care of others was always taught to me as being the number one concern. That is certainly at the base structure of many religions. And there is nothing wrong with it and I will continue to care, love and nurture others. But one thing this Covid-19 has taught me is that I matter, too. There is no question I have needed the rest as I am pretty sure many of you have realized as well. Working two and three jobs to make ends meet leaves little time for personal care and rest. Little time for meditation, self-reflection, and prayer.

Thus, it was on Kentucky Derby Day, as I finished up the last of the appetizers and was lighting the candles in the living room, I suddenly stopped. Looked around at the flowers, the food and paused to say a prayer of thanksgiving to God for providing me with such bounty.

As I turned around to finish lighting the candles, I felt a strong breeze waft across my face. This was a distinct and tangible feeling of wind against my cheek and believe me, there was nothing imaginary about it. Goosebumps skittered down my arms and back.

There were no windows opened in my house as all the windows were still sealed from the winter. The doors were shut. There was no cross wind.

In addition, I do not have central air and there are no overhead heat or air ducts that could have kicked on and erupted in a breeze. My house is nearly seventy years old and the heating system is "radiant heat" which was popular in 1950. The furnace is a boiler that heats water that then runs through copper pipes in the ceiling. The house is warmed by this "radiant" heat.

There was no way a cross wind or fan of breeze could have spun into life in that house.

That breeze was strong enough that it lifted my bangs and a lock of my hair, which is long. Not all that easy of a task.

Except one way.

An angel's wing.

That thought came to me like a flash. I did not know what to do. I did not see an angel. I did not hear anything more.

I stood in the middle of the room frozen and unable to take a breath, I said, "Who is that? And are you from the Light?"

Clear as a bell, I heard, "Yes. I am Michael."

It was Archangel Michael. He did not say that the wind or breeze that I felt was from his wing, but I intuited it. When these interactions and communications come to you; it is important to learn to feel their truth. Some of my friends who work with angels say that they feel a warmth all over. Some feel the warmth as a caring essence waft through their body. Another medium I know says she sees their colors. Michael comes in with blue lights and colors. (I agree on that one.) When there are more than one angel, many times it is a plethora of purple and lavender hued lights. I often see golden lights, almost like a liquid gold shower me. These are signs to help you understand and know that you are conversing with true angels and not imposters.

Imposters are from the negative forces. Some refer to them as tricksters. They have no real power and in fact they hover around weak individuals trying to steal that human's power. Unfortunately, too many humans think they are powerless in the face of evil. (Stop watching horror movies.) We are not. Tell them to go away in the name of God and to never come back again! And MEAN it! You have a voice. Use it.

As soon as I realized that Michael was with me, I felt my heart swell with gratitude. I said, "Thank you. Thank the Lord for me for this blessing."

I got no response in words, but a feeling/sensation of warmth filled me from the inside out and covered my body.

Being the emotional slob I am, I burst into tears. I was so moved, I felt weak in the knees. I looked in the long mirror on the wall near the door, half expecting to see the reflection of Archangel Michael in the mirror, but I did not.

All I saw was my reflection. Still crying. Still holding my breath.

And as I looked more closely, I saw my bangs, still askew across my forehead, right where Archangel Michael had blown them away.

Eleven

THE SECOND WAVE

Approximately six months after my visitation from the ten thousand angels, I had fallen into my same old, daily routine. Go to work, pay the bills, take out the trash. Rinse. Repeat.

Right? That is about all our lives. Maybe we can interject an occasional day when we have time to meditate in addition to an hour religious service on Sunday or a quick morning prayer. "Thanks, God. I got run. Kids to school, take the dog to the vet and get to work on time so I do not get docked in pay, or worse, lose my job." That about it?

What a grind.

And that grind is just the thing that causes my back muscles to tighten, hold lactic acid, cause pain and that again is repeated daily until I cannot take the pain anymore and I call for an appointment at the acupuncturist. I found my fabulous healer, who also happens to be a medical MD—an internist and one of the best. I've never been keen on pharmaceuticals to cure, re-direct energy or to solve my body's dis-eases and its lack of alignment with spirit.

I will go the holistic, natural, angelic route every time. This has seen me through quite a bit in my lifetime. I have used meditation, yoga, tai chi, healing bowls, Gregorian chanting, the full gamut of vegan, vegetarian, all-protein diets; fasting; exercise, neuro-linguistics, and hypnosis to cure everything from cancer to heart arrythmia. In my previous angel books, I have described most of these incidents in which the angels or a single angel has come to me in a dream and told me what I have had to do to be healed.

Suffice it to say, when my angels came to me in a dream and told me it was time to use acupuncture, I slammed on the brakes and said, "Yikes! Needles?"

Almost always, I am "good to go". Not this time.

Of course, an angel came a second time and repeated the directive. The next morning, I was in so much pain, I could barely breathe. I had no choice. I called the doctor and got an appointment for that evening after work.

My first visit was about a year after Jed died. Truth of the matter was that I was holding a lot of grief, sadness, and sorrow in just about every cell in my body.

My sessions over the next two years kept me healthy, boosted my immune system and allowed me to work ten-hour days at the dental office and miraculously pump out two to three novels a year and at least as many screenplays. What a blessing acupuncture is in my life.

By the fall of 2019, as I stated at the start of this story, I was no better off than the mindless gerbil running his wheel. I was overwhelmed with a glut of "physical world" issues and considering the intense pain in my back that was now shooting down the back of my legs making every stance torture, I had to get fixed and stay fixed.

As I drove to the acupuncturist's office, I had one of those visions of an angel's face who had come to talk to me. This can be very discerning when you are driving down the highway and BOOM! There is some glowing, gorgeous angel face smack dab in the center of the windshield.

Apparently, this guy/gal wanted my attention. I am not being flippant or disrespectful, but that is how it seems.

It was there for only a flash, so I was not in any real danger of driving off the road and making the headlines in the morning newspaper or on a cyber-newscast. What I heard was, "Reiki."

That was it. One word. Reiki.

For those of you who do not know, Reiki is a healing technique based on the principle that the therapist, (my acupuncturist) would then channel healing energy from the Universe by means of touch---or in the best of case, not touch me at all, and would then activate a healing process. Hopefully, the pain would be eliminated and a near-perfect balance of my energies would now flow through my body.

This was all well and good, except for the fact that the only Reiki master I knew lived in Houston, Texas and it would be months before I would be traveling to Texas and could get a treatment/session with him. Also, I live in a small town and even if there was a Reiki master nearby, this is NOT the kind of thing I would trust to a stranger. I am very particular about allowing healers into my aura and spiritual space. You never know if they leave behind some of their own spiritual/mental garbage that could leave me worse off than when I walked into their joint. At the very least, when looking for a spiritual therapist, Reiki master, acupuncturist, I would get as many recommendations as possible. I seldom get massages because I must trust the therapist.

The acupuncturist's office is on the far north side of town. It is situated on a large tract of land, surrounded by dense forest, and in the center of huge circular road is a lily pad covered lake. The lake is not large, like the ones with beaches, but neither is it small. I would say it covers close to ten acres. I am not good about sizes, but it was a large area, which is important for you to know. There are willow trees and pine trees, bushes, and cattails around the perimeter of the lake. The road is up on a hill and the pond is below. The road hugs the lake side and on the opposite side are a few commercial buildings. There is a great deal of space between the buildings.

I arrived at the acupuncturist's office and as she finished with her previous client, I went into the treatment room. By this time, we had become not just doctor and patient but friends. As usual, she would assess my current needs and situation by a brief interview. Therefore, when she asked me about my pain and emotional being, I blurted, "I had a visitation from an angel on my way here."

Fortunately, she knew about my angel books and I had told her about my contact and conversations with my angels.

She is a believer in much of what I shared with her and that helped my relationship with her and my trust in her as my therapist.

Interested in my comment, she asked, "What did the angel say?"

"He told me that I needed a Reiki treatment. So, I do not know what to do, because I do not know of a Reiki master."

She stared at me with a twinkle in her eye and a slow-growing smile. "I'm a Reiki master."

My jaw must have gaped. I had no idea. I had never seen a license on the wall. A diploma or whatever it is that Reiki masters hang. My friend had one in Houston.

She said, "In a few months, I'm actually going to take accelerated courses from a renowned Reiki master that I hope will help me to increase my ability to heal."

I was stunned. My angel came to me and told me that Reiki was the treatment I needed right now and I was certain it would be months before this would happen for me. Not a matter of minutes. "So, can we do this? Now?"

"Certainly."

She instructed me to lie face up on the massage table. I closed my eyes and the lights were dimmed, but not off. There was lovely Native American flute music playing. I love that music. Instantly, I felt relaxed.

She started at my feet. She touched my big toes and held them very gently. At the time, it seemed like forever that she remained at my feet, moving from the large toe to the smallest. A while later, she moved up my right side, barely placing one hand on my ankle and another on my knee. She remained there for a good ten minutes. She would lift her hands off my body and wave them over my body, but I had no idea what she was doing. She had told me prior to the start of the session that I should not talk and neither would she. It would interrupt the flow and the healing process. She placed her right hand on my knee and her left hand on my right shoulder.

She then repeated the process on the left side of my body.

That is when things started to happen.

While she had her left hand on my knee and her right hand on my left shoulder, I felt a third hand on my right foot.

The mysterious third hand held my big toe. Then touched the top of my foot. There was no way I was going to open my eyes, stop the treatment or talk. I was fascinated.

I wanted to see where this was going.

When she moved to the head of the table, she sat on one of the doctor's stools we all see our medical doctor use.

I kept my eyes closed, but now the "third hand" had released my foot and I did not feel it any longer.

She placed her hands on either side of my face and skull. She moved her hands over my forehead and did some other things, but to tell the truth my mind's focus was overhead.

My eyes were still closed. But in my mind's eye, I saw an enormous angel hovering over me. The angel was a good ten to twelve feet long and that wingspan filled the large room.

"You are protected."

I heard the angel in my head, not like a voice around the room, though it was very clear.

The angel wore a white gown and had white wings. It had blonde hair and blue eyes. This is important for you to remember when I relate my next story.

I did not receive the name of this angel. It did not give me a name.

I know my breathing was shallow and faint, almost as if I were not entirely in my body, using it.

The therapist continued to work on my head. I could feel her hands as she touched my ears. Then my cheeks.

The angel had no other words for me, even though I had dozens of questions in my head, I could not settle on one. I was flustered, and awed.

Suddenly, the session was over.

The therapy room that I was in has a glass wall overlooking the lake and wooded area I described earlier. There are those vertical long slat blinds that can be open or closed with a cord. The sun was setting and the slats were only slightly closed, so that I could see out into the lake and the trees.

As I sat up, fully clothed, and opened my eyes, I saw ten thousand angels, all dressed in white gowns. All with white wings.

The vision was only a flash, but long enough for me to see them spread their wings.

I heard the most beautiful angelic voice say, "We are here."

It was exactly like the vision I had seen of The Ten Thousand angels on the golf course only a couple months prior.

I was breathless. I did not say anything as I got off the table, looked back to the lake and saw nothing but water and the sunlight through the trees.

I sat at the little round table as my doctor sat opposite me. She asked how I felt.

Well, everything came gushing out. "First, I felt a third hand on my body! How is that possible?"

She smiled again, put her pen down and replied, "Did you now?"

That look of knowing told me volumes. "This has happened before?"

"Yes."

"Who is it?"

"One of my healing guides. They come in from time to time when someone needs special attention."

Uh, oh. I needed "special attention." "What kind of special attention? I was that bad off? Did I have a lot of blocks or is there something deeply amiss in my body?"

"Not really. I found a few blocks, but I removed them. Still grief and sadness."

I could so believe that.

Then she leaned forward and said in a low whisper, "There was something else, wasn't there?"

"I saw an angel. Flying right over me! I think it was the same one who wanted me to have a Reiki treatment."

"Ah!" She replied. "I knew it."

"You knew what?"

"I saw a crystalline presence over your body."

I was awed. Confirmation. Validation. "You did? What color was it?"

"White. I did not make out it was an angel, per se, but I felt it was."

"That is all I need to hear. Because when I sat up and looked outside, I saw the ten thousand."

"What ten thousand?"

I then told her about the ten thousand angels I had seen a few months earlier at my house. "All they said is that they are here."

Her face was very serious. "Did you ask why they are here?"

"No."

"You will see them again and you need to ask that. Ten thousand angels do not show up for no good reason."

I looked out the window to the lake. "This is a very peaceful place. A place of healing. Settled here amid all this nature, it makes sense they would come here. It is a portal for them. Just as is my house. I have felt that for a long time. That many angels are here for a reason. And I want to know what it is."

"So do I," she said. "So do I."

I had no idea it would not take long to get my next message.

TO BE CONTINUED

ARCHANGELS DESCEND

Author Note: I could not pinpoint the exact date of this next visit to my acupuncturist for a second Reiki treatment, most likely October or November of 2019.

Again, my back was a mass of very tight muscles. I had broken down and tried three or four massage therapy sessions and though the therapist was fantastic, they did not stick. I was working in the yard; cleaning out the garage for the coming winter; writing another screenplay or two and the long hours at the dental office mounted on top of an already tired and over-worked body.

Just as it happened the last time I had a Reiki treatment, I had made the appointment with a clear need to have an acupuncture treatment.

As I drove around that lovely lake, now surrounded by amber and gold autumn trees and gaggles of flying geese overhead, I heard a voice say, "You need Reiki."

I parked my car, turned off the engine and said, "Really? For real? What now?"

I was in pain and needed the body healing relief. But with this angel communicating to me, I suspected it was going to be the same message about the ten thousand angels. I felt I had already gotten that memo. But in my mind, I knew they were "here." That was their communique, though I did not understand exactly WHY they were "here." And what exactly did "here" mean? In my town? On the earth? Not in heaven? At my beck and call? What was going on?

I went inside and of course, my lovely doctor, was agreeable to the Reiki treatment.

This time as I laid on my back, eyes closed, I was surprised how fast I relaxed just to the music and her gentle touch on my toes. Perhaps it was because I had gone through this treatment before and knew what to expect.

Or so I thought. Boy. Was I wrong.

I would say I was about twelve minutes into the treatment, listening to the woodwind flutes, not thinking of anything, other than what was going on in my auric field that my angel would come to me and tell me that I needed Reiki. Granted, I had been very physical over the last two weeks and the body aches I had were warranted—just from the yard work alone. But I did not feel depressed, angry, sad or any emotion that I could honestly say had disrupted my aura. I did not feel anyone was psychically attacking me. Life was pretty much on an even keel. Lots of hugs at work. Lots of laughter with friends.

Then, in wide-screen cinemascope and Industrial Light & Magic CGI, stood a massively powerful Angel. He was brilliant, strong, and so handsome, I could only describe him as beautiful. There was nothing androgynous about him. He was male. He was a warrior and he was there with purpose.

He had thick dark brown mid-length hair that was not just shiny, it radiated. Everything about him radiated. He had olive almost tanned skin, brown eyes, and long lashes. His jawline looked like it had been finely carved by a sculptor.

His eyes were caring yet filled with knowledge, but the thing that struck me most was his intent.

He was easily fifteen or more feet tall. I know this because the ceiling in the room had dissolved. Above him was night sky with stars, planets, swaths of galaxies –as if he owned them.

His muscular arms rivaled any super star I have ever seen. From his wrists to nearly his elbows were gold cuffs that were carved with circular etchings that reminded me of the Gaelic carvings at Newgrange in Ireland. They were ancient in vibration. Around the ends of the cuffs were jewels.

Over his massive chest, he wore a gold breastplate. This, too, had precious jewels and stones around the neck.

Around his waist was a thick belt studded with jewels. And I mean a lot of jewels that shone as if they were lit by LED lights. (Which now, come to think of it, were they jewels? Or were they control buttons on an angelic cell phone?)

He wore a kind of "skirt" that was made of long gold pallets that hung from the gold belt and each ended in a pointed design. The ends of the plates or rectangular pallets were studded with jewels. Sapphires, rubies, emeralds, amethysts, gold topaz (?) orange topaz and diamonds. Later I realized they were all the colors of the human energy chakras.

He carried a gold sword which had a myriad of carvings and hieroglyphs on it. The hilt of the sword was set with jewels.

He was bare from his lower thighs to just below his knees where he wore some kind of gold metal shin guard and boots.

They reminded me of the armor that knights wore in the Middle Ages, yet they looked more ancient. These, too, had those circular carvings on them.

He leaned closer to me and it was then that his wings spread out and filled the room or rather the entire empty space because the room was not there anymore.

The room had dissolved, just like the ceiling had vanished or bled into the energy veil.

Rather than the white wings of the angels I had seen before, his wings were gold. Pure, glowing, powerful, radiant gold.

I was stunned and breathless. I think I stopped breathing at this point. I was not aware of the doctor's hands or the woodwind flutes.

I believe I had been transported to a different dimension.

I said, "You're Michael."

"I am. You know me."

"But I have never seen you like this. You have been coming to me all my life, but everything about you is so---transformed. Your wings are gold."

"This is my power. Touch my wing."

I touched the feathers of the wing and the feathers were soft. I had expected to touch metal, but they were just as you would expect a feather to feel. I was perplexed.

I just stared at the gold that lit the entire space.

"I came to tell you that God is pleased with you."

I was shocked. Awed. Humbled and started crying. "But I have not done anything. There is so much to do to save the world."

"That is why we are here."

"We?"

Michael backed up and to the left of me, a second Archangel descended. He was just as tall as Michael. Just as beautiful and equally powerful. He was extremely Gaelic looking. He had raven's wing black hair that was longer than Michael's. His skin was not tan at all, but not pale. He had deep Mediterranean-sea blue eyes and black thick lashes. His jaw was just as strong as Michael's but he had an impish gleam in his eyes.

He was bare chested, did not carry a sword and no breast-plate. He wore a kind of tunic with a jeweled belt around his waist. His arms were bare and he also looked like he could lift a couple dozen galaxies on a whim, just like Michael.

When he spread his wings, they were white.

This angel came to my left side leaned close and said, "I am Gabriel." He did not touch me, but said, "Remember me. I am with you."

The next angel was as tall as Michael and just as strong. The sheer magnitude of the power and force of their vibrations caused my teeth to tingle as if going numb. In fact, I was numb and electric all at the same time. It was a never-be-fore-sensation for me.

This angel had soft brown hair that was wavy and fell nearly to the end of his neck but not quite to his shoulders. He had the most incredible deep green eyes that would take a poet to describe. He wore a tunic but his had some kind of spring green scarf that flowed around his neck and fell down his back. The tunic was short so that I could see his bare legs. He had gold sandals that tied up to his knees with gold lacings.

"I am Raphael." He said it like "RAH FAYEL."

"I've seen you before."

"Yes. When your heart was breaking. But I fixed it. It is important you remain whole in the days to come."

At that moment I was so stunned by what was going on, I did not pick up on the ominous undertones of Raphael's words.

The fourth angel appeared right in the middle of the others as if he had shot down from heaven in a bolt of light and wind.

He was blonde as a Scandinavian god of lore, light blue eyes and a flowing tunic and robe of a diaphanous fabric so white it blinded me.

This angel was the first that felt feminine, though he had a man's face. His arms were covered by the tunic and the fabric swirled around at his feet, so I never saw his feet.

He came over to me and waved his hands up and down my body and said, "I am Ariel. I am here to heal you. There is much to do."

"Heal me?"

"We have to make you lighter."

"Lighter? I need to diet?

"You need to watch your diet, but no. We are increasing the frequency of your energies."

I did not know what to do or say other than, "Okay. Whatever you need to do is fine with me." I was giving them permission to use me as the instrument of the Lord for whatever He wanted of me.

The session with Ariel did not last another five seconds. And just as he arrived, he left. Straight up into the heavens, he zoomed.

Raphael and Gabriel simply faded.

Michael was the last to leave.

I said, "What do you want me to do?"

"Believe. Trust in us."

"But I always do."

"It will be more difficult in the days to come to hold the faith."

"Why?" At that point all I could think was that I was going to die. Something was going to happen to me and this was my early warning to get my act together. Do something for the planet. Do something for those I love? I did not know.

Reading my mind, he said, "No. You will not die. You will help us."

Then it hit me. "You want me to write about this visitation."

"Yes. But not now."

"Why not?

"It is too soon. It will not be long. We will tell you when to write and what to write."

"As you always do," I replied.

"This will be different. The needs of the people will be different. There will be much fear and you will need to

assuage their fear. NO MORE! There can be no more fear. That is what is wrong with the earth. Humans have been trapped in fear, anger, and hatred too long. They make my job more difficult."

"I am sorry."

"You will tell them this: Love. Do not judge or hate. When you dream, those moments are real and powerful. Dream of peace. Send love and peace to the earth. Forgive everyone and everything. The earth will be made new."

"How new?" I had no idea at the time what he was talking about.

"We will show you over the coming days."

"I'll do whatever it is that you want," I promised.

"Talk to us and we will talk to you. It is God's will. Remember that. All that transpires is God's will."

"I'll remember."

"Love and peace," he said and vanished. Just like that.

I cannot begin to explain the void I felt when he was gone. It was as if I was whole, filled with a love and comfort I had not felt since my last near-death experience. God's love was all around me and now it was gone.

No wonder it is so hard for humans on this earth. That separation from God is horrific. It bends the mind to all manner of dark places. Even anger at being cast away again.

It is so hard to keep believing when we do not have a daily dose of an angel's visit or God showing up in one way or another to remind us how precious and special, we are to someone.

And that someone is the One Source. Our Creator. God.

Twelve

BACKTRACKING

I *have always given credit to the angels and my divine* "muses" for the novels I write. From my first historical romances over forty-five years ago to the present romantic thrillers and adventure romances, the stories come to me as if on angels' wings.

A good deal of this book has been channeled or rather downloaded from the divine. Believe it or not, it is difficult for me to say that out loud. Not that I feel it is boasting, but sometimes, I get a bit freaked out by the things that happen to me. This morning I got up and thought that this book was finished but my angels came in and said, "Not quite." I am to relay to you the following three stories.

1985-1987.

During this time, I lived in Houston. My son was in middle school. I worked at our family spa and swimming pool business, but two days a week I took the mornings off to write. I would go to my exercise class, come home, shower, meditate; and before I started to write my novel, I went to my computer and commenced to contact the divine forces through automatic writing. They referred to themselves, as "The Group." I asked if they were from the Light, (from God) every day and always got the affirmative "Yes."

Their messages always began with affirmations of their love and protection for me and my family. They confirmed their own guidance came with aid from Archangel Michael. They advised me to read the Gnostic Gospels, the Gospel of Thomas, The Books of Enoch and more. I also read every book about Edgar Cayce that was in print.

The pertinence of this information being presented in this book thirty years later is that I was given specific predictions and warnings about the future. Those messages were often shocking and terrifying.

I was told that I came to earth to help with the "ascension." I had no idea what this meant since the only person I knew about in history who had ascended was Jesus. Of course, today there is a great deal of talk in the spiritual community about humanity evolving; the Ascension to the New Earth; the planet itself ascending; and ascending to the fifth dimension or higher.

They told me that in the future, there would be a "shift."

Since I was reading Edgar Cayce's books and his predictions about 1999, I concluded that the shift must be regarding the shift of the North and South Poles that Cayce spoke of.

They told me there would be a "schism" in Christianity at the turn of the century and in the years following that would cause many to lose their faith. They also said that those who lost their faith, "never possessed true faith." They said that those who were most traumatized were ones whose faith was based on dogma and false teachings.

They showed me visions of earthquakes, floods, tsunamis, and hurricanes that looked like the end of the world.

They foretold of many deaths from disease like a pandemic, but I dismissed this one out of hand. In 1985, we had had the "swine flu" but I could not imagine something taking over the whole world that science and medicine could not cure. It never dawned on me that the "flu" would be man-made or that bio-weapons would become prevalent.

Back then they told me that the people on the earth would become very fear-filled. This fear was almost intractable. Hatred would span the globe. I saw a dark web cloak the earth and the people on it, as if an evil spider had spun that sticky web. People had lost their ability to think and discern. They appeared not to notice the existence of this web, but walked around in it, like robots.

I was given a vision in which we had no electricity, heat, or gas to run our cars. We were struggling for our lives in the future. The scene was so frightening to me that I immediately quit the automatic writing. I questioned whether the information I was receiving was accurate and true. I had not experienced dark messages from angels prior to this. Now, I did not trust this "Group." Maybe they were tricksters.

All my life I had believed goodness could be found in every person. I always believed that people were inherently kind, even if their "walls" were up or if their coping mechanisms were questionable.

When I looked at the future filled with evil persons, untrustworthy leaders and political systems that wanted total world domination and that looked far too much like Nazi regimes of the past world war, I wanted to run screaming.

I took all the books that "The Group" had told me to read, though I had, indeed, read them; and donated them to my local library.

For me, seeing the dark place that society and humanity had devolved to was not acceptable. I was determined to do everything I could to "flip" it around. In addition to praying for the world to see God's love and mercy in every aspect of our lives, I kept my writing focused on up-lifting, happy-ending romances. I threaded mystical, spiritual elements into the plot lines as much as my editor-at-the-time allowed.

2024

Presenting my last story to you about Michael and the other archangels appearing to me and the message that Michael delivered about the earth's dire present predicament—the message I received this morning was that this has been coming for a long time.

We have been warned time and again.

The timelines of the earth's future have changed many times over the millennia. *The timelines can be changed by our prayers and especially by focused and active meditation.* Human beings have done it before. Do not listen to those who tell you that you are powerless in the face of this pervasive evil.

We have to TRUST that we have this power and TRUST the divine to alter the trajectory of our timeline.

NOW, we must believe in our POWER as human beings that we CAN change the world and make it peaceful, loving and kind.

BI-LOCATING

The following two vignettes illustrate the types of untapped powers we all have within us. We have the power to be telepathic, psychic, intuitive and self-healing. We are capable of "moving mountains." Until we become aware of our own abilities and admit to owning these gifts, we remain stagnant pawns in someone else's game. We should all be the heroes of our own play.

My Story.

Bi-locating is the ability to physically be in more than one place at the same time. Angels and other dimensional beings do it all the time. Chances are a great many of us did this in childhood. Maybe you remember having dreams of flying. Or traveling to a friend's house to play, when your mother would swear you were taking a nap or playing by yourself with Legos in your bedroom.

This incident occurred to me only three years ago while I was still working at my brother-in-law's dental office.

I had gone to the eye doctor and told Sandy, the receptionist, that I would only be gone about an hour. One of my friends was sitting in the reception area waiting for her appointment.

As Sandy tells the story, about twenty minutes later, I drove into the parking lot. My friend, the patient, looked up from her book and said to Sandy, "Oh, look. Cath is back early. She just drove into the parking lot."

Then, I walked into the inner reception area where Sandy sat at her desk. Sandy said, "Cath, you are back early. Did you forget something?"

"No," I had said and continued walking into my big office.

Sandy went back to her computer and answering the phone. The patient was taken to the back operatory to have her teeth cleaned.

Another twenty minutes or so passed and Sandy answered the phone. It was me calling. I said, "Sandy, I just finished my eye appointment and I'm on my way back."

Sandy was stunned. "Is this a joke?"

"What are you talking about?" I asked.

"You are already here. I saw you come in and go to your office."

Now it was my turn to be shocked. "That is impossible. I just got in my car."

Sandy put me on hold, went into my office and saw that I was NOT there. She came back to the phone. "Cath, I am not crazy. Our patient saw you as well."

When the real me drove back to the office, I not only discussed the strange event with Sandy, but with the patient as well, who swore she saw me plain as day drive into the parking lot and park my car. She said I had the same clothes on.

This is the only incident I can remember as an adult of bi-locating, but as a child I used to tell my mother how I went to someone else's house for dinner or to play. THOSE play times that I experienced are as clear as my memories of a few minutes ago.

I cannot bi-locate at will.

What I do know is that I am capable of this power, this transcendent ability. I am human. I am still discovering my spiritual self.

LEVITATING

No, I never studied with yogis, Zen masters or chi masters. I have not the slightest clue how to make myself levitate at will and I do not particularly feel this is necessary in my life.

However, the following is simply a demonstration of another "power" that we humans inherently possess. It is just that we do not know it.

We have been so dumbed down by society, religions, political systems, and propaganda media that we go around in our lives like hamsters on a wheel.

I know I am ready to get off that wheel and get on with my "real" life.

2002

I was on book tour for my novel, *The Christmas Star*, when this incident occurred.

My publisher drove us from Illinois to Indiana, to Ohio where we participated in morning drive-time radio and television shows and then attended book signings later in the day.

In Cincinnati, we shared a room in a nice hotel after a long day of interviews and a book signing. We had enjoyed a good dinner and I was exhausted. I fell asleep upon hitting the pillow.

The next morning, my publisher asked, "How did you sleep?"

"Like a rock," I answered.

"Really? No nightmares?"

"No," I said wondering where this was going. "Why? Is something wrong?"

"Kind of. Last night I got up to go the bathroom and you were levitated two feet off the bed."

"What?"

"You didn't know that?"

"I have never done it before. I do not think." I had to really ponder this.

I was immersed in a some very esoteric reading, going back to those Gnostic Gospels and such, but I sure was not taking levitation lessons. I was, however, deeply immersed in spiritual matters.

As human beings we have so many spiritual powers that we do not know about and certainly do not access. However, we can.

Along with these powers is our ability to negate hatred, war, revenge, anger, and negativity in the world. Send your light and love to every cranny and corner of the earth. Use your God Spark to make the change to a better world which is our **Divine Right.**

Thirteen

I have compiled these stories over several years and as you can see many of them were written prior or during the Covid-19 pandemic. The world will never go back to the way it was. Nor should it. There were and are a great many things amuck about our societies, governments, institutions, industrial military complexes and corporate monarchies that need to be altered or completely bulldozed into the past.

What has amazed me is that during this time, I had integrated nearly all the messages that the angels had given me and their guidance has become a way of life for me. I send light and love to every living being on this planet every day. I have gathered around me all those who do the same. We are a powerful group of everyday people who focus on the positive and who believe that our main purpose for being on the earth at this time, this given day (and were not taken during the pandemic), is to fight with our love for the higher consciousness of humanity. If we can send space shuttles to far away planets, why can't we reach for the stars in our own lives? Why can't we dream of a world with no war?

What is the good of fighting? No one wins in war except those who make money off the sale of war goods. It is all about the money. Not patriotism. I hope we are finally seeing the light in that regard.

Love will win.

I said at the beginning of this book that we live in a simulation. A matrix and we can get out of it. We are energy beings, who take on the matter of these bodies to come to earth to experience a great many things.

Our energy will live on. We will ascend to the next dimension and the next. We may go all the way back to Source and be one with Source energy. We will all live forever. We are part of Source and the God Source is immortal. It is infinity.

HOW do we break out of this matrix box and this simulation, you ask. Prayer is one way, but it is petition and too often, in our pleading, our fear of not being answered comes through. We are not as active in prayer as we can be.

Meditation is the most powerful tool available to us. That is right. My angels come to me with blaring trumpets and banging drums to get my attention and the message is always the same. Meditation. I am not talking about meditation that simply relaxes and the next thing you know, you have fallen asleep in a chair.

I mean meditation that involves focus, intention, visualization, and projection of an outcome. These four **actions** are crucial to the results you seek---that of freedom from this bondage. The more you put into the meditation, the more you will get out of it. You are in control here. You have the power.

To best describe this kind of meditation and how I accomplish this, I am going to walk you through a very focused and active meditation.

I try to carve out a good half hour to do this in a peaceful, silent setting. Admittedly, there are times when I will spend an hour sending light and love to the world.

Start out in a comfortable position and drop into your breath. Really pay attention to your breathing. Inhale through the nostrils. I always see golden, diamond light coming down from The Creator into the top of my head, or crown chakra, surrounding my entire body. This is not only protection from any and all negativity, but it is also healing. I inhale this for a count of ten, all the way down to my belly and hold for the count of four or more. Then exhale. I do long, lung emptying exhales as if getting rid of any kind of negative residue that is there. I do this three times.

To really go deep, I envision myself walking down a spiral staircase of 99 steps. This takes a while. As you start out, the more detail you can put into it, the more you will exert your imagination and visualization abilities to bring you results.

Pay attention to your feet. Are you barefoot? Shoes? Sandals? What are you wearing? Pajamas? Suit? Gown? What color? Are you carrying a candle? A lantern? A flashlight? Is there light around you? Is it white light or are there colors? What is the source of the light? Sconces on the walls? I've seen ancient torches with burning fire sometimes.

Are the stairs concrete? Marble? Carpeted?

Now count the steps. See the numbers on the steps. Do they change color? Turn to shiny gold? Brilliant diamond?

Has anyone/angel/friend left anything on the steps for you? Gifts? Is it something symbolic? Flowers, perhaps. What kind? What color? A single flower? A bouquet? Do you hear a voice telling you to pick up the flowers?

Do you see food, perhaps. Drink? A key? What kind? Do you have an impression of what it unlocks? A car? A door? A safe? Jewels? Is there a book? What is the title? Is it sacred writing? A children's book from your past?

Keep counting down the steps. See the numbers on the steps as you descend. Sometimes a specific number will bring in a symbol. 44, 33. On step 33 one time, I saw a crown of thorns. A booming voice told me not to pick it up. That karma had already been paid. Number 19 is Archangel Michael's number. Sometimes Michael may be there. He may or may not lead you the rest of the way.

At the bottom of the steps is a door. Or double doors. What is it made of? Wood? Gold? Glass? Crystal? Stone? Is there a latch? Gold? Silver? Brass?

Is the door open? Cracked open? Is there light coming through? Is it sunlight? Moonlight? Colored light? Is it closed tightly? Can you open it?

As the door or doors open, where are you?

Walk into this new dimension. It is not earth. Where are you? It could be a garden. Seaside. Another planet. A Forest.

Are there trees? Any animals around? Do they talk to you? Are there birds? Do they sing? Are there mountains? Clouds?

Sky?   Sometimes you will see a crystal city. A futuristic city. One moon or two?

A person is coming toward you. Watch as they approach.

This person is luminous. It could be an angel. It could be an ascended master. Or this person could be your higher self. You are meeting you.

Ask this figure if they are FROM THE LIGHT.

Wait for the YES answer. If they do not answer, they are an imposter or a trickster. Tell them to go away and never come back again.

Then wait for the Being of Light to appear. Ask if this Being is from the Light.

Then, once that YES is established, ask what messages the Being has for you. You will feel an awesome gratitude. Your heart will swell with love for the Universal Love you are receiving from God. You may cry. Have goosebumps. Your emotional reaction should be strong as you feel this angelic, all-consuming love. You feel comfortable and you trust this Being or Angel.

When you awaken you will write this down.

Now, the Being will take you to a conveyance of some kind. Could be a car, a small space pod; a hot air balloon.

You will rise upward until you are above planet Earth. From this highest point you will send LIGHT AND LOVE to every living human, animal, plant, drop of water, the earth, the sky everything that is in your consciousness as your human reality. Your heart will expand with the love you can share.

The love you send will *nullify* the hatred, violence, jealousy, greed, and negativity that has created a dark web of enslavement in the 3D reality.

See all warring nations experiencing a change of heart. See guns turn into flowers. See children with enough food and water that there is no want. See barren lands brimming with lush crops. See the seas crystal clear. The air clean.

With each visualization **you** are creating this New Earth. Let your imagination take you where you need to go and be. Create your perfect world.

Slowly, you will ease yourself back to you waking/normal state. You will remember everything you did and what was said to you.

Many times, the angelic messages are simple. Such as, "Pray for the earth."

When you finish, make sure you say THANK YOU to your angels and your Higher Self. Gratitude is so very important. It is one of the highest and most powerful frequencies in this or any dimension. I have stated this in every one of my Angel Watch series of books. THANK your angels for protecting and guiding you. YOU may not be paying attention to them, but they never stop caring for you. Start every day in gratitude thanking God/Source for being alive one more day to be the light of the world that you are, to make these changes. You have one more day to love.

And love will win.

Love is all-powerful. We can create it every day. It can start with the tiny seed of an act of kindness for just one person. That person is you. When you look in the mirror in the morning, tell yourself you love you.

Then go out there into your world and say exactly that to someone else. Each time you throw that pebble of kindness out there, it creates that fantastical, beautiful continual, ever-pulsing ring of loving energy that lifts the vibrations of every person that person sees, everywhere they walk, and imbues their thoughts throughout the day with positivity.

You can be a light unto the world. You do not have to be a preacher, teacher, or pod-show host to alter the currents of fear that snake through the ethers around this earth. You can discharge a great many negative vibes by simply smiling at people when you walk down the street or wave to someone in traffic rather than snarling at them.

Remember the old saying, "The buck stops here?"

In this post-covid world, fear is having a heyday.

It would be so simple for all of us to give in and give up.

When America was facing her darkest days two generations ago, President Roosevelt said, "All we have to fear is fear itself."

Winston Churchill said, "Never give in – never, never, never, never, nothing great or small, large, or petty, never give in except to convictions of honor and good sense. Never yield to force; never yield to the apparently overwhelming might of the enemy." He said this in 1941 at a speech at Harrow School. It is as valid today, maybe more so, than ever before. Never give in to the enemy. Fear is our enemy.

As I stated in the first story in this book, I learned that day in New York as I read in the USA Today newspaper that Americans believe in God and miracles.

As humans we pray. We pray in many fashions and formats. It is inherent in our souls to acknowledge our divine spark. Even when we disavow the divine, we are admitting there is something there to disavow.

We will always hope…and fight. Both are part of our will to survive as a species.

We will believe in our angels and work with our angels to make a better world for ourselves and our children and our grandchildren.

Our human loving hearts have always come to the rescue of each other and those in need around the world.

We have courage. It is ingrained in us. All of us, even the least of us.

That means you and me. We must fight fear with love. We can envision a new timeline with a golden new world, of peace and equality.

This world right now is at a tipping point. Are you choosing peace, joy and love or fear, hate and revenge?

You make those choices every moment when you buy into the unfounded fear manipulations being pressed upon all humanity by those who see us as slaves.

You do not think that is true? You think that is some political stance of mine? Go back to the last chapters and re-read what the angels told me verbatim over the last five years.

Humanity MUST not buy into fear. At any cost.

Humanity MUST stop this hatred.

Humanity MUST stop anger. We will not survive a nuclear war.

Jesus said put away your sword or you will destroy yourself. Isn't that warning enough?

Pay attention to the small and big signs that the angels and messengers of truth and love are telling you.

Are you paying attention yet?

THE END

Angel Timelines

BIBLIOGRAPHY

Alexander, Eben. *Proof of Heaven*. Simon and Schuster. New York. 2012.

Alexander, Eben. *The Map of Heaven*. Simon and Schuster. New York. 2014.

Blavatsky, H.P. *The Land of the Gods*. Radiant Books. New York. 2022. (Original Publishing Date 1887. "An Adventure Among the Rosicrucians.")

Braden, Gregg. *The Divine Matrix: Bridging Time, Space, Miracles, and Belief*. Hay House Publisher, Inc. Carlsbad, CA. 2008.

Braden, Gregg. *The Isaiah Effect*. Sounds True. Audible. 2001.

Cannon, Delores. *Horns of the Goddess*. Ozark Mountain Publishing. Huntsville, AR. 2022.

Cannon, Delores. *Jesus and the Essenes*. Ozark Mountain Publishing. Huntsville, AR. 2009.

Cannon, Delores. *Three Waves of Volunteers and the New Earth*. Ozark Mountain Publishing. Huntsville, AR. 2021.

Cannon, Delores. *The Convoluted Universe*. Ozark Mountain Publishing. Huntsville, AR. 2019

Canova, Peter. *Quantum Spirituality*. Bear & Company. Rochester, VA. 2022.

Carson, Billy. *The Compendium of The Emerald Tablets*. Coral Springs, FL. 2019.

Chionetti, Alex. *Mysteries of the Tayos Caves*. Bear and Company. Rochester, N.Y. 2019.

Cosme, Sarah Breskman. *A Hypnotist's Journey to Atlantis*. Copyright 2020. Sarah Breskman Cosme. 2020.

Hancock, Graham. *Visionary*. "Mysterious Origins of Human Consciousness. New Page Books. Newburyport, MA. 2022.

Hurtak, J.J. *The Keys of Enoch*. Academy for Future Sciences. Los Gatos, CA. 1979.

Hurtak, J.J. *Pistis Sophia*. Academy for Future Sciences. Los Gatos, CA. 1999.

Ike, David. *The Dream. The Extraordinary Revelation of Who We Are and Where We Are*. APG Books. Herndon, VA. 2023.

Kovacs, Betty. *Merchants of Light: The Consciousness That Is Changing The World*. The Kamlak Center. 2019.

Lumpkin, Joseph B. *The Books of Enoch: A Complete Volume Containing 1 Enoch (The Ethiopic Book of Enoch)*. Fifth Estate, Incorporated. 2011